Sweet Blessings,
Wanda S. Markey/Holmes

CHAPTER 1:
GET OUT

"Child abuse casts a shadow the length of a lifetime."

- Herbert Ward

"Take that illegitimate kid of yours and get out!"

Those were the first words I ever remember hearing from my daddy. I didn't understand the words, as a four year old at the time, but I will never forget his anger. The year was around 1950.

Daddy had a bottle in one hand, the other hand was clenched into a fist. "Let that jerk of a dad take care of his own kid. I only took her in because you married me. Well I've had enough. You can both hit the road!"

I didn't realize that my little brother, Ronnie, belonged to my step-dad, therefore, he was never banished from the house. I didn't even know that he was my step-dad, he was the only daddy I knew.

He screamed at Mama, slapped her across the face, then back handed her on the other side. He gave her a shove and ordered us to get out.

"Come on, Wanda," Mama said, "Let's go."

Mama grabbed a hold of my hand. Daddy didn't even let us get a coat before he slammed the door behind us. We hid in the dark

DADDY NEVER CALLED ME PRINCESS

shed that cold, windy night. There wasn't even a full moon to give us some light. Mama cried. I was freezing and I couldn't stop shaking. I was so scared. My nose started bleeding, again. Mama didn't even have a rag to stop the bleeding. She dumped one of the rabbits' water dishes and held it under my nose so I wouldn't cover myself in blood.

A long time later Mama tip-toed around the house, with me holding tight to her dress, and peeked in the window.

"Okay," she said, "he's passed out now. We're safe. Let's go back in the house."

Home to us was a two-car garage on thirty acres that Daddy converted into a house. Dividers were put up to make a kitchen, a living room, and two small bedrooms. One bedroom for Mama and Daddy. Another bedroom for my little brother, Ronnie, and me to share. We had a set of bunk beds. We didn't have wooden doors, the openings were covered with old sheets sewed onto a broomstick and nailed above the doorway. Since we didn't have indoor plumbing, we used a pot which Mama surrounded with a curtain for supposed privacy. Water was pumped from a well and we could only take sponge baths.

Mama used her talents, and lots of hard work, to turn our meager house into a home, complete with green ruffled curtains and starched white doilies.

My warm bed felt so good as Mama tucked the covers under my chin and kissed me on the cheek. "Good night, sweetie," she said. "Get some sleep. Things will be better tomorrow."

But nothing ever changed, at least not for the better.

Mama wasn't too happy when I had to start school, she just wanted me to stay with her, so sometimes she kept me home. Daddy didn't know I missed so much school, he wouldn't have liked that, so we didn't tell him.

I made friends with Darcy, from my kindergarten class, but I wasn't allowed to have her over. I wouldn't have wanted to anyway. I

GET OUT

was too embarrassed about things that happened at home. Darcy was a good friend at school, when I did go.

"Why do you wear the same clothes all the time?" Darcy asked me.

"They're the only dresses I have, but Mama washes and irons them, so they're clean."

"Oh, I know," she said, "and your dresses look nice, but I have a lot of clothes, maybe I can share with you. I'll ask Mother."

Mama got a phone call from Darcy's mother. "Would you be offended to accept a bag of Darcy's clothes? She has more than she needs and Darcy and Wanda are about the same size."

"Well no," Mama said, "we'd appreciate them."

The lady dropped the clothes off and I had so much fun going through the bag. "Oh, look at this yellow dress: it has lots of ruffles and a big bow in the back. Can I try it on now, Mama? Daddy will think I look pretty."

Mama helped me into the dress and fixed my hair so I could model for him. When I walked into the room Daddy took another swig from his beer bottle then looked up at me.

"Hey, Wanda, you look like a movie star." He laughed. "Yeah, Lassie. You look like you combed your hair with an egg beater."

My stomach started hurting again.

Maybe I'd make Daddy happy next time, I thought, but next time never came. I couldn't understand why. I used to think maybe he didn't like me because I had dark hair, not bright red, naturally curly hair, like Mama and Daddy. Even my brother, Ronnie, had thick red hair. He was the spitting image of his daddy who was tall and slim. People said Ronnie would probably be just as tall. But then again, none of us ever made Daddy happy. Not even the baby Mama had when I was five, a little girl named Rose. They nick-named her Penny, because her hair was as red as a copper penny. And least of all, Mama, five foot two, eyes of blue. Everyone said she was a real

DADDY NEVER CALLED ME PRINCESS

looker.

Mama's good looks were passed on to Penny. By the time I was in first grade my little sister was toddling all over. She had a head full of bright red ringlets and an adorable smile. She laughed all the time, except when Daddy looked at her real mean, then she'd start crying.

"Well, look at that," he'd smirk, "she's going to cloud up and rain all over."

Ronnie made Daddy the maddest of all. Mama said they were both so stubborn. Ronnie did things he knew he wasn't supposed to do and Daddy always found out. Like the time Daddy came out of the outhouse cussing and yelling. "Ronnie! Get out here!"

Oh no, he found out that Ronnie threw his train down the hole.

Daddy dragged Ronnie to the outhouse. He held him upside down by his legs and made him reach through the mess. Ronnie screamed and gagged till he found his train and pulled it out. "Now go get cleaned up." Daddy told him.

Ronnie was terrified of the dark so Daddy locked him in that dark little shed out back. Ronnie wouldn't have had to stay there if he'd promised not to be bad anymore. Mama said he just wouldn't give Daddy the satisfaction.

Ronnie kept screaming. "Help, help, let me out!"

Daddy let him scream for a while then he opened the door and said, "Okay, do you think you can be good now?"

Ronnie stopped crying only long enough to stubbornly say, "No."

All he had to do was say, "Yes," but he refused.

Daddy slammed the door and locked it again. Even in the house you could hear Ronnie's screams. The pile of empty beer bottles got bigger until Daddy passed out on the couch. Mama opened the door and let Ronnie out so he could come in and go to bed.

GET OUT

Daddy didn't usually hit us kids. "You might get away with slugging me," Mama would scream at him, "but you will not hit one of my kids!" But we saw what he did to her and we were all terrified of him. He'd scream and make us think he was going to clobber us.

"Now you get in there and sit on the bed," Daddy's voice would boom, "stay there and think about what you're going to get when I get in there."

Just dreading our punishment for hours was pure torture. The torture only lessened when he headed for the nearest bar. Mama spent time alone with us when Daddy was gone. We'd have fun playing "Hide the Button." Sometimes we'd hide it so good that no one could find it. "Well you can't hide it where none of the button even shows," Mama would say.

But playing "Beast, Bird, or Fish," was my favorite. The person who was it would say either beast, bird, or fish, then they'd point to someone. The other person would have to come up with the name of a beast, bird, or fish, before the first person counted to ten real fast. We'd all try to see who could count the fastest, even if the little ones couldn't get all the numbers right.

Sometimes Mama played the guitar. She used a knife on the strings, instead of her fingers. She also had a small keyboard and played, *"Black Hawk Waltz,"* one of my favorites. We loved to sit around and listen to Mama sing old Indian songs and recite poems.

On Saturdays, when Daddy didn't have to work, he needed quiet so he could sleep. Mama would send us outside to play until lunch time. I remember one Saturday. We were all playing outside and I was starving before Mama came after us, "Hey, kids, lunch time."

We headed into the house to eat our peanut butter and jelly sandwiches. We walked in to the smell of steak and mushrooms, so we knew Daddy was up. It smelled so good, but since Daddy worked hard all week and needed his nourishment, it was only for him.

DADDY NEVER CALLED ME PRINCESS

Ronnie walked over to his dad and stood there staring at him, watching him eat.

"Well, Lyle," Mama said, "he wants a little taste of your steak."

"If he wants a bite of my steak then I'll give him a bite."

Before Daddy gave him a piece, he took his bottle of hot Tabasco sauce and shook some on the meat. Ronnie took the bite. He started choking and yelling. "It burns, it burns."

Mama got Ronnie a glass of water and helped him drink it. "That was a mean trick," she told Daddy. "He'll never ask you for another bite."

"Well that was the whole idea." He laughed "Maybe now he'll leave me alone and let me eat in peace."

We only had peace when Daddy's car pulled away. Laughter rang through our house when he was gone. At least until he pulled back in the drive and everything came to a halt. Headlights shining in the bedroom window, or the sound of keys in the door, jolted us awake. Daddy would stumble into the house and bark his orders at Mama.

"Hey, woman, get out of that bed and cook me a steak."

Poor Mama would follow his orders, climb out of bed, and light a fire under his steak. I'd pray that he wouldn't hit her. I never knew how long I'd be able to stay in bed after the fighting started. Voices would get louder and louder until I'd hear the slaps. Soon thereafter I'd hear Daddy's hateful words, "Take that illegitimate kid of yours and get out!" The same scene played out many times over.

But for all the love we never got from Daddy, Mama tried to make up for it when he was gone. "You kids are my whole life," she'd say, "I couldn't stand it if anything happened to any of you." Then she'd try her best to think of fun things to do that didn't involve money.

Us kids also liked to come up with our own fun things to do. We knew she'd let us do anything we wanted, if we asked her enough times. There was a favorite place we liked to hang out, but sometimes the place got us into trouble. We'd do something bad and get caught. We knew we'd need a lot of begging before she'd let us go, so we all started in at once.

"Can we go Mama? Can we, can we? Please...?

CHAPTER 2:
GOLF COURSE HAZARDS

"One of the advantages bowling has over golf is that you seldom lose a bowling ball."

-Don Carter.

"Okay, you can go," Mama told us. "But you all better behave yourselves. I don't want to see you riding home in the back of a police car."

Our thirty acres had trees on the property and a huge apple orchard right next door. We could walk straight out back and we'd run into a golf course that sat just beyond the trees. That was our favorite place to hang out. We loved the smell of the golf course, and running on the soft grass with our bare feet. We had fun rolling around on the greens, watching the clouds roll by. Until some golfer hollered and interrupted our day dreaming, then we had to jump up and take off. Otherwise, we might have gotten whacked in the head with a golf ball, maybe not even accidentally.

We heard the golfers talk about golf hazards, like the sand traps and the lake where a lot of their shots ended up. There seemed to be special rules if one of their balls landed in a hazard.

But, back then, there was also another type of hazard: three little kids, ages 8, 5, and 3. We figured out that by hanging around the golf course we could get our hands on a little extra money. Even if that meant annoying the golfers, and stealing. We'd hide behind the maple trees and watch everyone play. Golfers said the

DADDY NEVER CALLED ME PRINCESS

green was fast when a light stroke to the ball made it roll a long distance. Whenever a golfer hit his ball a long ways off Ronnie would run over and pick up the shot. The fast green gave us more time to get away. We'd sneak over to the cleaning machine and wash the dirt off. We'd save up a few balls. Then we'd take them to the golf course and sell them back to the players. The money provided for more trips to the corner store, our favorite place for penny candy.

Our stash of golf balls was large enough to start selling. Ronnie was the salesman, people seemed to take pity on such a cute, freckle faced little boy, most of the time. Penny and I were the watchers in the bushes. Ronnie was trying to make the first sale of the day.

"Hey, mister, would you like to buy a golf ball?"

The man took the ball and looked it over. He shouted at Ronnie, "Hey, this is mine, you kids stole my ball!"

Ronnie took off running. "Let's get out of here!" he yelled. We followed him and the mad man was right behind us. We managed to escape when the golfer gave up chasing three little kids full of energy. We ran home to hide in the house.

"Hi, Mama, we're home."

"Why are you kids all out of breath," she wanted to know, "what did you do now?" She wasn't too happy when we told her what we did. "You kids are going to get the police after you one of these days, I keep telling you! Then your dad is going to kill you."

Home was still a nice safe place to run back to. Anytime we walked in the door we could count on Mama being there with a welcome, and that's where we headed, especially when we got into trouble. And we knew that Mama's banana bread would be coming out of the oven at any time.

Our neighbor, Harry, worked in a grocery store. He brought us the lettuce, day old bread, and old brown bananas that were going to be thrown in the trash. But Mama made good use of all the overripe food. She could make the best banana bread. There were

GOLF COURSE HAZARDS

even times I liked the day old bread. Like the time Daddy sent me to bed without any supper. Mama waited til Daddy passed out, then she brought me a piece of that day old bread, with butter, and nothing had ever tasted so good.

After eating some freshly baked bread, we went back outside to play. Ronnie wanted us to play golf at home. Since we didn't have any golf clubs he decided to use a baseball bat. Ronnie wanted to be the first one to swing and we were waiting on the side lines. I'm not quite sure how it happened, but his fly ball missed it's target and smacked me right in my belly button—it took my breath away. That had never happened to me before and I didn't know why I couldn't breathe.

"Hey, Mama!" Penny yelled. "Wanda got hurt."

Mama came and checked me over. "Oh, you just got the wind knocked out of you," she said, "you'll be okay."

But I didn't feel okay, my stomach was killing me. I decided, right then and there, it was the last time I was ever going to play golf, at least with my brother and his homemade hazard.

But, there was something else we loved to do, not to make money, just to have fun. We had been warned to keep away from the area, several times. But we loved the place so much that it was hard to keep away. We called it our secret hide-out. Should we listen to what Mama said? Could it really be that dangerous?

CHAPTER 3:
ONE BROKEN OAR

"It's a good idea to begin at the bottom in everything except in learning to swim."

-Author Unknown

    We were warned to keep away from the water. We weren't even allowed to go to the golf course for awhile, after the trouble we got into last time. We told Mama we wanted to take a walk and gather some pretty leaves because we needed them for school.

    We promised her we wouldn't go any farther than the edge of the woods that day, even if someone hit a long shot that was just waiting to be picked up. But that was okay, we weren't desperate for candy. Us kids had just went Trick or Treating for Halloween. We had each carried our own pillowcase and walked around the country side for miles. We got so much candy it was almost too heavy to carry back home. But we managed.

    So on our promise she let us go off for our adventure in the woods. The day was beautiful, one of the last warm fall days. We didn't even need a sweater. At first we did pick up a bunch of pretty, colorful leaves. We came to the edge of the woods and we could see the golf course. If we walked a little farther we'd come to

DADDY NEVER CALLED ME PRINCESS

the lake, right in the middle of the golf course.

We'd been warned, but we just wanted to look. We set our bags of leaves down and started out of the woods, onto the golf course.

Sometimes we went to the water, each of us dragging a homemade fishing pole from the long branches we found in the woods. We didn't use bait, we'd just sit at the edge of the water and pretend we were fishing. We didn't tell Mama that part.

We kept walking until we could see the lake. There was an old abandoned boat, sitting along the edge of the water. The boat looked like it would be just big enough for three.

"Hey," I said, "Do you want to just sit in the boat and see how it feels?"

So we all climbed into the creaky old boat. I felt pretty daring and excited.

"Why don't we just drag it closer to the water and float out a little ways?" Ronnie said, "we can pretend we're fishing."

"That sounds good to me." I said. "You stay there, Penny, and we'll give you a ride." Ronnie and I climbed back out of the boat. We pushed and pulled on the old thing until we were out deep enough to float. We climbed back in the boat. There were a couple of old empty coffee cans under the seat, for some reason, and one broken oar. Floating around the water and watching the fish swim by was fun. Ronnie was trying to catch bluegills with his hands.

"Be careful, Ronnie," I said, "or you'll fall in. None of us know how to swim." Suddenly Penny screamed, "Look, the boat's leaking!"

Sure enough, water was seeping into the boat. We were far from shore, in water so deep we couldn't even see the bottom.

We couldn't paddle back to shore with only one oar. We took turns with the empty coffee cans, or even our hands, trying to dip the water out of the bottom. The faster we dipped, the more water came in. We were all soaked and the water was rising at a

ONE BROKEN OAR

surprisingly fast rate.

There was not a soul in sight. Penny started to cry, "We're all going to drown."

"Don't cry," I said, "we'll be alright." But I wasn't so sure. I knew we should have listened to what we'd been told. My heart started beating faster. Partly because I was working hard, but mostly because I was scared. And I wasn't the only one, although Ronnie would never admit that he was afraid.

We heard voices in the distance; the voices got closer. We were happy to see Mama and one of the neighbor's walk up to the shore. I was so glad to see them, even though Mama looked panic-stricken.

What in the world are you kids doing out there?" she yelled, "get back here this instant."

"We can't," I hollered, "we only have one oar and it's not all there."

"The boat's leaking!" Ronnie yelled.

"We're sinking!" Penny cried.

I didn't know how Mama was going to help. She couldn't even swim. And she was deathly afraid of water, ever since some mean boys tried to drown her when she little. But Mama surprised me. She jumped right in the water, along with the neighbor lady. "We're coming kids," the neighbor hollered.

"You kids just sit down and keep still," Mama screamed. They both managed to get close enough to grab the boat. Maybe the water wasn't as deep as it seemed to us. They pulled us back to shore. I was so happy when we stepped back on dry land, I could have kissed the ground, like I saw them do on television. Although I dreaded what we'd get at home. But Mama was so relieved that none of us had drowned, the only thing she gave us was another warning. Daddy would have made us sit on the bed for hours, dreading our punishment, or worse. Mama promised not to tell him about our scary trip with the rugged rowboat and one broken oar.

DADDY NEVER CALLED ME PRINCESS

I know she didn't want Daddy beating on her kids.

"I take enough beatings," she'd say, "for all of us."

She tried to cover her black & blue marks with make-up but it didn't always work. Mama had a hard life. She only wanted someone to love her. I wondered what we were going to have to do next, to prove that we loved her.

CHAPTER 4:
WHO LOVES ME BEST?

"Life is tough enough without having someone kick you from the inside."

- Rita Rudner

"Hey, kids, I'd like an apple. Who wants to get it for me? Remember, the one who gets it first, loves me the most."

We all loved Mama. We'd race to the kitchen trying to prove that we loved her the best. We spent a lot of time looking for different ways to make Mama feel loved, and I knew, that as much as she was able, she loved all of us. But I could tell that she hadn't been acting like herself. Something was wrong. She'd be real sweet one minute, and in the next breath, she'd scream.

"You kids are driving me crazy!"

She seemed to get upset over every little thing.

She was tired all the time. She fell asleep any time she sat down. And, oh yeah, she threw up every morning. Then we found out why. She was going to have another baby.

She apologized for the way she'd been acting. "I'm sorry kids, it's just these hormones."

We told her it was okay and that we forgave her. We were

DADDY NEVER CALLED ME PRINCESS

excited over the new baby on the way. Penny and I wanted a little sister, Ronnie wanted a brother. Mama said she didn't care, just as long as the baby was healthy.

She grew larger with each passing month. With us kids on the couch, gathered around Mama, we'd put our hands on her stomach to feel the baby kicking. We were amazed.

"I'm so tired," Mama would say, "and my legs are swollen."

We didn't have foot stools, so she asked us if we'd hold her legs up. She'd sit on the couch and we'd take turns standing between her feet, holding her legs up in the air. She enjoyed it so much that it turned into a nightly ritual.

"Remember," she'd say, "the one who holds them up the longest, loves me best."

We'd all argue, wanting to be first. Then we'd try to outlast each other by holding her legs up the longest. She appreciated our acts of love. Daddy never did, no matter how hard we tried. Mama said he never felt love as a little boy, so he didn't know how to show, or receive love, from any of us. The beatings didn't even stop while she was pregnant. I couldn't understand why she stayed with him. One time, he even got mad because she was too tired to get up & cook his steak. He took the large porterhouse steak in the bedroom and kept slapping her across the face with it, screaming, "Get up and cook this steak, get up and cook this steak!" So who loved her best? It certainly wasn't Daddy. So we tried to show her that we loved her. And Mama loved us back. She always noticed her kids and made us feel important, especially on our birthdays, and one of us was about to have a party.

CHAPTER 5:
PARTY TIME

"Today was good. Today was fun. Tomorrow is another one."

— Dr. Seuss

"If it's not fun, forget it."

That should have been Penny's quote. With her sparkling personality she was like a party just waiting to happen. Pleasing Penny was easy. Any kind of a celebration would make her happy. We were planning a surprise for her fourth birthday.

Mama never had money for gifts but we always had cake and ice cream. Daddy was a Master Electrician and he earned a good pay check, he was even working a lot of overtime, but we saw very little of his money. Mama said he spent most of it in the bars and on new cars. Many a time Mama took all of us kids out the back door, whenever bill collectors came, to hide in the woods.

But all of our birthdays were made special and we felt important, like we mattered. Mama would decorate the house and fix a special meal. We'd eat on the picnic table, weather permitting, in the back yard under the big oak tree. Everyone would gather around and we'd have fun playing games, singing and telling jokes. We'd even put on pretend plays, or puppet shows.

DADDY NEVER CALLED ME PRINCESS

Mama needed help for Penny's surprise. My job was to keep Penny busy while Mama got everything ready. Ronnie took off down the road to visit a friend. I took Penny outside. We played school and I was the teacher. A couple of empty beer cases made some great chairs, even if they didn't smell too good. Rusty old TV trays that were rescued from the neighbor's trash made great desks. Penny drew pictures with several pieces of broken crayons. Pretend home work, of writing the numbers from one to ten, was assigned. After she got tired of that, I read her favorite Little Golden Book to her, "Pokey Little Puppy."

"Is my party ready yet?" Penny kept asking. I was hoping it wouldn't be too much longer. Penny was getting harder to entertain and I could hear thunder in the distance. A storm was headed our way so we were going to have the party inside that day.

"She'll let us know," I told her again, just as the door opened and Mama came out. She was wiping the sweat off her face with her apron, and she still looked good. Mama always kept herself looking nice. She fixed up and wore make-up every day. I planned to do the same thing if I ever got married.

She sat down under the tree with us. "Isn't Ronnie back yet?" she asked, "I told him not to be gone too long. Everything's all set, just as soon as your brother gets back we'll go in." We were listening for him to come down the road. Every time we heard a noise Mama jumped up and looked down the road. "Here he don't come," she'd say, just trying to be funny and get us all excited.

Penny spotted him first. "Here he comes," she yelled as we all went out to meet him.

"What took you so long?" Penny asked. "My birthday party's all ready."

"Well, I'm here now," Ronnie said, "Let's go." We all started back to the house. Penny ran ahead. Her naturally curly, bright red pony tails bounced in the breeze. Her long green hair ties were swinging. She looked so cute in her plaid dress with the puff sleeves and white buttons down the front. We had to hurry to catch up

PARTY TIME

with her. Mama opened the door and let the birthday girl go in first. Penny's blue eyes sparkled with excitement. Her favorite thing: A party, just for her.

Red, yellow and green balloons, tied with thread, hung around the living room. Mama had a big sign taped to the wall, "Happy Birthday, Penny."

The table looked pretty, set with Mama's few pieces of china. She could thank Duz laundry soap for that. Hidden inside each box of Duz was a piece of fine china, decorated with a golden wheat pattern and gold edging. She had spent many months and was still trying to gather her collection. She only used it for special occasions.

Mama's little touch of loveliness, in a harsh world.

The silverware collection on the table also came free: hidden, then pulled from boxes of another brand of soap. The forks and spoons even looked good resting on a folded up paper towel. Rising from an empty jelly jar, in the center of the table, were three longed stemmed red roses, picked from her garden. Everything looked colorful and inviting.

We took our places around the table. Chilled glasses of strawberry Kool Aid were poured into red, blue, purple and gold Aluminum Tumblers. The glasses once held cottage cheese and were delivered to our door by the milkman. Mama had asked Penny what she wanted for her birthday dinner, but we knew she'd pick pizza. We all loved Mama's homemade pizza with Polish Sausage and cheese. Yummy smells filled the room as pieces were passed around. We could hardly wait to sink our teeth into a big slice. We devoured every last bite.

Then we sang the most popular song in the world,"Happy Birthday," to Penny. She made a wish and blew out all five of her candles. There was always one extra candle on the cake. "And one to grow on," Mama would say.

Penny made the first cut in the chocolate cake, with white

DADDY NEVER CALLED ME PRINCESS

frosting, that she'd asked for. Big pieces were put in bowls for each of us. Every slice was topped off with a large scoop of chocolate ice cream, then drizzled on top with a squirt of Hershey's Syrup.

Mama hauled out her guitar and played for us. We tried to sing along to "Roll Out The Barrel, We'll Have a Barrel of Fun." We spent the rest of the evening playing hide the button and other games. We didn't need presents. We had each other, and that was enough. Laughter rang throughout our small home until it was time to get ready for bed.

And we knew that another birthday was coming up, but it wouldn't be near as much fun. The next birthday was going to be Daddy's. I wondered what Mama was going to make us do for him, trying to show a love that didn't exist.

CHAPTER 6:
LOOK DADDY

"A merry heart maketh a cheerful countenance: but by sorrow of the heart the spirit is broken."

- Proverbs 15:13

Daddy's birthday. "Here's some money," Mama said, "you can all walk to the corner store and pick out some birthday cards for your Dad. And when you get back, it would be a nice surprise if you'd all clean his car while he's sleeping in."

So we all walked to the store, got our cards, walked back home and got to work on Daddy's birthday surprise. Ronnie got all the pails for water; Penny hunted up the wax and I gathered up a bunch of old towels.

"Well, the best thing you can use," Mama said, "is lots of elbow grease."

"Elbow grease?" Penny asked, "where's that?"

Mama laughed and grabbed Penny's elbow, "Right here, just scrub hard."

Penny wasn't big enough to do much scrubbing, but she tried her best. We all worked hard on that hot July day. We washed the dirt off the car, then used towels and dried it real good. We put the wax on and let that dry to a haze. Then we polished the car to a

DADDY NEVER CALLED ME PRINCESS

sparkling glow. Daddy always drove new cars, they were his pride and joy, and he liked them clean and shiny. We were all sweating and scrubbing and I knew he would be pleased when he saw his car. It would be worth it all, no matter how hard we had to work, just to see Daddy's face.

We were sitting under the shade tree waiting. Mama brought out glasses of cold strawberry Kool Aid, then she went back in the house to tell him we had a surprise outside. He finally came out, holding his coffee cup. He took a sip then walked over to look at his car. We were all watching his face. He walked around to the front of the car and inspected it all over. He walked around to the other side, took another swig of his coffee, then walked to the back. Daddy looked towards all of us, then pointed to a place on the car.

"You missed a spot. Right here." Then he turned around and walked back into the house.

I couldn't believe it. After all the hours of hard work in the hot sun: not so much as a "Thank-You," or even a smile. Ronnie and Penny looked as disappointed as I felt.

Mama wasn't feeling well but she came outside again. She looked so tired. "Oh my, that looks good, you kids did a great job."

"Thanks, Mama." If only those words had came from Daddy. We all went back inside. Mama wanted us to sing "Happy Birthday." He opened his gift of Old Spice aftershave, then he opened our cards. Ronnie saved his for last. On the front of the card it said, "Happy Birthday to someone who is always my best friend." When you opened the card, it said, "My Dog."

Daddy wasn't too happy when he looked at that. *"Oh, no,"* I thought, *"what's he going to do to Ronnie now?"*

CHAPTER 7:
OUR FIRE PIT

"Children need love, especially when they "do not deserve" it."

-Harold Hulbert

Ronnie had a close call that time. I thought sure he was going to get it good over the birthday card he gave his dad. But Daddy only glared at him for what seemed like ages, then he shook his head and took off for the bar. Penny would have been in tears under the evil looking eyes, but Ronnie was too stubborn, just like his dad.

Ronnie, Penny, and I spent the rest of the afternoon playing outside. Along towards evening we heard voices coming from next door. Since we lived in a rural area with lots of open space, we could see the close neighbor's. They were sitting outside in a circle, gathered around their fire pit. We could see long roasting forks and the smell of hot dogs wafted in the air. Sound travels in the country and we could hear them talking. "Hey, whaddya want on your hot dog?"

"You know what I like," she said, "just give me the works, and don't spare the onions." They even had marshmallows and I heard a voice, "Make mine toasted nice and brown."

"That looks like fun," Penny said.

DADDY NEVER CALLED ME PRINCESS

We all watched with a longing that we could do the same, but we didn't have a fire pit. That was about to change. I came up with what I thought, at the time, was a great idea. *Us kids could make one of our own.* "Hey, don't you guys wish we had a fire pit?" Convincing Ronnie and Penny to help me build one was the easy part. Mama probably wouldn't be coming out to see what we were doing, she'd just holler and check on us from inside.

We went out back, so she couldn't see us from the house. We got Daddy's shovel and started digging. We all took turns until we had a hole about as deep as one of Daddy's beer bottles. We wandered around by the creek until we found enough stones to lay around the edges.

"Ronnie," I said, "do you think you can walk around and find some twigs for our fire?"

"Sure," he said, "I'll get a bunch of them. And I'll grab some lighter fluid out of the shed."

"Penny, come with me. I'll hunt for some matches, if you go get some of Daddy's old newspapers to start the fire."

Ronnie headed out back and Penny and I went in the house.

"What are you kids doing out there?" Mama yelled from the living room.

"Nothing," I said, "just watching the neighbors."

"Well, don't you kids be bothering them now," she said.

I found some matches and stuck them in my pocket. "We won't," I yelled on my way out.

Penny grabbed a stack of Daddy's old Flint Journal newspapers for me to crumple. Ronnie arranged the twigs on top in the form of a teepee. It was almost dark as we huddled around our creation. I poured on some lighter fluid, struck the match and threw it in the middle. Flames shot up so fast that Ronnie even got his eyebrows singed. The fire was so hot it could have burnt the feathers off a chicken.

OUR FIRE PIT

After things settled down we enjoyed watching the sparks climbing the night sky. The neighbors didn't have anything over on us; or nothing except hot dogs and marshmallows. *How can I get my hands on something for us to roast?* I wondered. We couldn't walk to the store, it was too late. Besides, our stash of empties was low. Daddy had returned some of his own bottles, so the pile wasn't big enough for us to sneak any that wouldn't be missed.

Suddenly, bright headlights and a car pulled in the drive. We all froze in sheer terror.

"Daddy!" We shouted in unison. "What's he doing home now?" We quickly doused the fire with our handy pail of water, then walked towards the house as if nothing happened.

What can I tell Daddy? I better think of something good.

Daddy stomped right over to us. I almost wet my pants.

"What in the blazes were you kids doing out there?"

"Oh, we were just playing with a flashlight," I said.

"A flashlight, my foot!" He screamed. "Don't lie to me! You were playing with fire. Don't you kids know any better than that? Do I have to tell you everything? Now get over here, all of you. I'm going to give you a spanking you'll never forget."

Was Daddy going to start beating on us now, like he beat on Mama?

Mama heard all the commotion and came running outside. She couldn't run too fast, with the baby inside her almost ready to be born. She was all out of breath, holding her big belly.

"You're not going to hit them!" she said.

"Well they've got to learn that they can't play with fire!"

Daddy pulled off his belt. Mama couldn't talk him out of it. I got whipped first, then Ronnie, and Penny was last. We got our first spanking ever, from Daddy. Penny and I walked to the house crying. Ronnie refused to.

DADDY NEVER CALLED ME PRINCESS

"Now you kids get over there and sit on the floor," Daddy said, "and be quiet! You got what you deserved."

"Hey, Reta," he hollered, "throw that steak on and bring me a cold one."

We didn't get to enjoy our fire. We had to spend the rest of the evening sitting on the floor, watching Daddy guzzle down one beer after another. We not only didn't get anything to roast, but we had to sit there with growling stomachs and watch Daddy eat his steak and give us the evil eye, daring us to say a word. We couldn't even watch Lassie, one of our favorite shows. If we had a dog like Lassie, maybe she would have protected us from Daddy and his belt.

Maybe, I thought, *if we begged Mama enough, she'd ask Daddy if we could get a puppy. I know he didn't think we deserved one, he was always telling us we didn't deserve anything. But maybe, if we promised not to make any more fire pits?*

CHAPTER 8:
LASSIE & THE LITTLE ONE

"The horse is prepared against the day of battle: but safety is of the Lord."

- Proverbs 21:31

"Please, Mama. Please...Ask Daddy if we can get a dog?"

But every time we asked, we always got the same answer.

"We barely have enough food to feed all of us. We certainly can't afford dog food."

Lassie was one of our favorite shows. We especially wanted a dog like her. Lassie was a hero and always protected Timmy. I'd day dream about all the adventures they had. Even at night, I'd dream about possible adventures that we could have with our very own dog.

Then one day while we were outside, to everyone's surprise, a stray dog wandered up to us. The dog was so pretty, a beautiful full grown collie. I couldn't believe my eyes: she looked just like Lassie.

"Be careful," Mama said, "you don't know anything about that animal."

But the dog came right up to me. I reached out and touched her thick fur. "Look, Mama, she's not mean, she likes me." I hugged the

DADDY NEVER CALLED ME PRINCESS

soft fur on her neck. The dog let all of us pet her.

"She looks hungry, can we feed her something?" I asked.

"I guess we can spare a couple pieces of that day old bread."

I found an old dish Mama said I could use and I gave the dog some water too.

"Can we keep her, Mama?" We all chimed in.

"Well, a nice dog like that, and so well cared for, I'm sure she belongs to someone. Don't get too attached. Her owners will probably come looking for her."

I wanted to tie her up, so she couldn't run away, but Mama wouldn't let me.

"She found her way here by herself," she said, "maybe she can find her way back home."

Lassie seemed to like me best of all. She followed me everywhere. Lassie would sit when I told her too, and she knew how to fetch a ball. When we played hide and seek, Ronnie and Penny would hide, and Lassie would stay right beside me. We'd go looking for them together.

I'd hurry outside every morning to see if she was still there. I'd hug her neck and she'd lick my face while I talked to her. "Are you still here?"

That's the same thing the neighbor lady would holler at Mama when she saw her outside.

"Are you still here? I thought you were supposed to have that baby last month?"

"So did I," Mama told her, "I'm over three weeks past my due date."

Whenever I'd been around Mama and her friends all they ever talked about was the horrors of childbirth. One woman said she was in labor for four days. I pretended not to listen, but I heard every word they said. I was so worried about Mama, and I prayed really hard.

Then one morning Mama started having pains. She couldn't get a hold of Daddy.

"I need to get to the hospital," Mama said, "The neighbor can take me, but the baby sitter can't come for a while. Do you think you could watch Ronnie and Penny till she gets here?"

"Sure, I can watch them, we don't need a baby sitter. I'm old enough, I'm nine."

"Well, you're not old enough yet, but I don't have a choice. So you all stay in the house and wait for her. Don't let them play with matches. Don't let them handle any knifes. Just sit on the couch and watch TV, or read, or something."

"We'll be fine, Mama, just get to the hospital."

"You two mind your sister," she said, as she walked out the door with her suitcase. I was feeling so important, being the baby sitter, but it didn't last long. I heard someone pull in the drive. I figured it was the baby sitter so I ran outside. Ronnie and Penny followed me. A black truck was pulled up close to the house. A heavyset, old man with dirty coveralls, large glasses and a beard was walking towards us. I backed away, but he was suddenly standing so close I could smell his beer breath.

"Hey, are you kids all alone here?"

"No, my Daddy's in the house," I said.

"Well, I don't see his car anywhere."

Then, out of nowhere, I heard a low growl. Lassie was there, between us and the stranger.

"Whoa! Keep that dog off of me." The man said.

Lassie moved herself tight against me and kept growling at the man. The stranger backed away slowly, reached behind himself and opened the door of his truck. He jumped in, turned on the key, and stones flew as he backed out the drive.

DADDY NEVER CALLED ME PRINCESS

I hugged the dog with trembling hands. Ronnie & Penny hugged her too. The collie had protected us, just like the real Lassie. I could hardly wait to tell Mama what happened. I knew she'd be so happy. Certainly, after she found out, she'd let us keep her.

But Lassie suddenly pulled away from our arms. She took off running towards the road, chasing the man's car. We called and called, but she wouldn't come back. We ran out to the road and watched until she was out of sight. There was nothing more we could do. We all went back in the house and I wondered if we'd ever see her again.

Not long afterward the baby sitter showed up. I didn't want to go to bed that night. I was worried about Mama. But the baby sitter promised to come and wake me up when she heard any news. Hours later the phone woke me up and I jumped out of bed and ran to the living room.

"Your mom and the baby are both doing fine. Your dad said he was going to stop at the Cozy Corner Bar on the way home, to celebrate."

Ronnie got his wish for a brother. Mama got her wish for a perfectly healthy baby and she named him, Rodney. We could hardly wait to see him, but kids weren't allowed to visit in the hospital. We had to wait until Mama brought him home.

A few days later Daddy brought Mama and Rodney home, but he wasn't so little. He weighed nine pounds and ten ounces. Mama said that's because he was a ten month baby. He could finish off a whole bottle in no time. He looked just like Ronnie, with bright red naturally curly hair. But Mama said his temperament seemed more gentle and easy going. Even though Penny and I didn't get a sister, we both fell in love with little "Rod." Daddy kept his feelings to himself, whatever they were, he just seemed in a hurry to leave.

"Hey, Reta," he yelled, "I'm going to run up to the corner, be right back."

Daddy came home carrying something behind his back. He

handed Mama a bunch of pretty flowers, all different colors. Mama looked at the bouquet and gave Daddy a dirty look.

"Well, if you can't bring me any flowers from the florist, then I don't want these weeds that you picked along side of the road."

She threw all the flowers in the garbage. Daddy just shook his head and laughed.

"I'm going to run up to the Cozy Corner for a quick one." He said, then he walked out.

Daddy never helped with anything, not even a diaper change. I was Mama's little helper, even if that meant I had to stay home from school. I didn't mind. I hated school, but I loved helping with the baby. He smelled so sweet after his bath, and I'd kiss his little hands and toes.

Rodney only cried when he was hungry or needed to be changed. When I'd sing to him or read him stories, he'd fall right to sleep. Rodney was an easy going little guy with a sweet disposition. We'd sit around in the evenings and take turns holding the baby and loving on him. Since she had Rodney, Mama was like her old self again, she even got her smile back.

Mama made all of us smile that night when she made her delicious goulash for supper. Just having a baby didn't slow her down a bit. We even had banana creme pie for dessert.

Then we all sat on the couch and watched television with our bag of goodies to snack on.

Daddy's car pulled in the drive early that night, before the bars had even closed. Someone flipped off the TV. We almost tripped over one another scrambling to our bedrooms. Mama even ran and got in bed. We heard keys jingling. The door creaked open and Daddy stumbled in.

"Hey," he hollered, "everyone get back in here. I know you're not asleep. You left swinging drapes and a warm television."

We went quietly back in the living room. There was a big bulge

DADDY NEVER CALLED ME PRINCESS

under Daddy's coat.

"Here," he said, "I brought you something."

He unzipped his coat and set a little blond puppy on the floor. She was adorable. Daddy said she was a Cocker Spaniel.

"Now, you all better take care of her. I don't want to see any messes in this house either. You can keep her outside."

We all agreed. Then we played with the puppy and let her lick us all over. I wanted to name her Trixie and everyone liked the name. We finally had a playmate. She might not have been Lassie, but little Trixie was all ours. We could teach our dog how to fetch and do tricks. We could make her a dog house. But she couldn't live on day old bread. She'd need something just for her. *Maybe,* I thought, *if we didn't get caught, we could sneak a few more of Daddy's empties and trade them if for some real dog food.*

CHAPTER 9:
SORROWS CAN SWIM

"People who drink to drown their sorrow should be told that sorrow knows how to swim."

- Ann Landers

"Hey, Wanda, get me another beer."

And when Daddy had company on the weekends, it was, "Hey, get us a couple of beers."

I was used to it. I'd been Daddy's little waitress ever since I could remember. I was probably around ten years old at this time. After Daddy and his friends left, us kids would sneak a few of the empty bottles and set them aside. We couldn't take too many, or he'd get suspicious.

"Hey," he'd yell. "Where are all the empty bottles? I know I drank more than that."

So, for every three or four bottles that Daddy and his friends drank, that meant another empty in our hidden stash. But they added up, until we had enough to walk to the corner store, a mile away, and return them for two cents each. We'd have enough money for either potato chips, pop, or a bag of penny candy. We'd take turns on who got to choose our goodies, to go along with the evening's entertainment of games and television. Or, sometimes, we'd just devour ice cream on the way home.

One day, Penny and I bagged up a load of empty bottles and

DADDY NEVER CALLED ME PRINCESS

took off walking to the store. Before we made it even half way, our trip was stopped cold. Coming down the middle of the road, straight towards us, was a bull. We were terrified when the huge monster snorted and pawed the ground. Bottles flew everywhere and we heard the sound of breaking glass.

"Come on Penny. Quick!" I yelled.

She started crying. I helped her and we both scrambled up a huge lilac bush.

"We're going to be fine," I said. "Mr. Smith must not have fixed his fence. He probably doesn't know his bull got out yet. But, I'm sure he'll come looking for him any minute."

We were both shaking. Fear kept us clinging to the lilac bush. The bull stood between us and the candy we wanted, and he didn't look like he was going to leave. There weren't any houses nearby, so we couldn't scream for help, and Mr. Smith was nowhere in sight.

After starting to think that I couldn't hold on any longer, the bull turned and wandered off. As much as we loved candy, Brahma the bull sent us running down the dirt road, as fast as our little legs could go. Forget the candy, I just wanted the safety of Mama and home.

Even with all the money that the empty bottles provided, I hated passing out beer to the smelly old men. They'd look me over, wink at me or try to touch me. Some of them would even scratch my hand when they took the beer, if Daddy wasn't looking.

The men were disgusting, so I tried not to get too close. Whenever Daddy had company I stayed in my room. I did a lot of reading, or writing, between beer calls.

Daddy had friends over one night. I was in my bedroom when Mr. Cliff came in.

"I'm going to run up to the corner for another six pack," he said. "Do you want to ride along? I'll get you kids some candy."

When Mr. Cliff mentioned candy, my ears perked up and I ran

SORROWS CAN SWIM

to the kitchen.

"Can I go with him, Mama? Please?"

"Well, if he's just going to run up to the corner and right back, then I guess it will be all right."

I climbed into his truck. Daddy was in the outhouse when we pulled away. I didn't know why, but after we started down the road, I felt afraid. I stayed way over on my side of the truck and held on to the door knob. Mr. Cliff was talking and laughing.

"What kind of candy does your brother and sister like?" he asked.

"Ronnie likes black shoestring licorice. Penny likes the candy buttons, so she can rip them off the paper."

"So what do you like best?" he asked.

"Well, I like the red candy lipstick."

"Oh, I do too," he said. "That's my favorite."

We pulled into the store. I picked out some candy for all of us kids. Mr. Cliff picked out some extra candy and threw it in with the rest. He got his six pack and we headed home. I couldn't wait to get back and show them the bag of candy I was clutching on my lap.

He was driving real slow. I kept my head turned, looking out the window and watching the trees pass. The sun was going down and it was hard to see, but I kept looking. There was a dead deer lying at the edge of the grass, all mangled and twisted. I wondered how long it had been lying there, it's body game for other animals.

About half way home, Mr. Cliff stopped and pulled off to the side of the road.

"What are you doing sitting way over there?" he said. "I won't bite."

"That's okay," I said. "I'm fine. I like it over here. I always ride close to the door."

DADDY NEVER CALLED ME PRINCESS

He just laughed. Then he reached out with his huge hairy arms and pulled me over next to him.

"Do you like to kiss?" he asked.

"Well, I kiss Mama," I told him.

"No," he said. "I mean a kiss from a man, like this."

He pulled me closer and put his face against mine. I could smell sweat and his beer breath. His whiskered face scratched mine. He clamped me so tightly I could barely breathe. When he rammed his tongue in my mouth I almost threw up. I couldn't push him away but when he backed off I started to cry.

"My daddy's going to come looking for me if I don't come right back."

We saw headlights. Mr. Cliff shoved me back over and started the truck. I was never so happy in all my life. It wasn't Daddy, but at least it had scared him into taking me home.

"Don't tell your daddy anything about this," he warned. "Or you'll be in big trouble."

"I won't," I said. *At least until I get home*, I thought.

When we walked up to the house, I could hear Mama and Daddy fighting.

"Now why in the world did you let her go with him?" Daddy yelled.

"Well it was just up to the corner," Mama said. "I figured it would be okay."

I was too scared to talk about it in front of Daddy, so I didn't say anything right then. After Mr. Cliff and Daddy left, I told Mama all about it.

"Well, that filthy old man!" she said. "They're all a bunch of dirty old drunks. Try to stay away from them, from now on. I'm going to tell your dad just what kind of a friend he has."

SORROWS CAN SWIM

When Daddy came home that night, Mama told him what his so-called friend did to me. Daddy was furious and said that he was going to pay Mr. Cliff a visit. We never found out what happened during that visit, but none of us ever saw or heard from Mr. Cliff again.

I felt safe and protected by Daddy that night.

But, as best I could, I kept my distance when Daddy's drinking buddies came around. I was starting to learn what they really wanted.

Sometimes, if no one showed up, Daddy would take Mama out dancing. We'd stay at home with a baby-sitter. I didn't mind, because I loved to see Mama go out and have a good time. She loved it, and she deserved to have some fun. She'd put on a pretty dress, long dangling earrings and high heels with lots of straps. When she kissed us good-bye she smelled like Ta-bu.

I didn't have to fend off drunken old men: girls baby-sat for us, so I felt safe. Since I was the oldest, I got to stay up later. We'd watch television and eat candy until it was my bed time.

"Get in there and brush your teeth now," the babysitter would tell me.

"Oh, we don't have to brush our teeth," I'd say. "Mama says they're our teeth, and if we don't want to take care of them, then it's up to us."

"Well, if you don't take care of them, you're going to have a bunch of cavities the next time you go to the dentist."

"I don't have to worry about that either, none of us ever go to the dentist."

"You're kidding," she said. "With all that candy you kids eat, you're all going to pay."

I didn't care, at the time. Whenever Mama and Daddy would fight, or I'd be afraid, I'd just reach in that little brown sack of comfort, all that candy, so many choices, and I could disappear for a

DADDY NEVER CALLED ME PRINCESS

while.

Daddy had a craving for the bottle, but I had a craving for what the empties provided. We both needed an escape. Sweets helped me cope with life. Candy helped me to forget, for a little while, all the dangers that seemed to lurk behind every bush. But I wondered what Daddy was trying to escape from. I never could have imagined what I was about to find out.

CHAPTER 10:
ICE CREAM CATASTROPHE

"Memories are bullets. Some whiz by and only spook you. Others tear you open and leave you in pieces."

- Richard Kadrey, *Kill the Dead*

"I want to sit by Mama."

"No, I do."

"Okay, you don't need to fight about it," Mama said. She put Ronnie on one side, Penny on the other, and Rodney got to sit on her lap. I sat on the end. We were all gathered on the couch, dressed in our comfy pajamas. We wanted to snuggle up next to Mama and her fuzzy green robe. She wanted to tell us something important.

"This is going to be hard," she said, "but I need to tell you a story about your dad. You're always asking me why he's so mean. Maybe this will help you understand why he acts the way he does. But how about we all get a bowl of ice cream first?"

"Yeah," we all agreed and headed for the kitchen. We had Neapolitan in the freezer so we could each have some of our favorite flavor. I liked a little of each kind. Mama dipped up a bowl for everyone and I took my first bite. "Yum, this is really good. How come Daddy never eats ice cream?"

"Well," Mama said, "that's part of what I'm going to tell you. But let's sit at the table and finish our ice cream first. Then we won't make a mess on the couch."

DADDY NEVER CALLED ME PRINCESS

Ronnie liked to stir his ice cream until it was soft, like a milk shake. Penny copied him. Mama gave Rodney spoonfuls of her ice cream. We heard oohs and ahhs as everyone enjoyed their favorite flavor. Empty bowls were put in the sink, hands and faces cleaned off, and we returned to the couch.

"Okay, now," Mama said, "back to the story. I want to talk about memories, some good and some not so good."

"Like the time Wanda made a fire and Daddy spanked all of us?" Ronnie asked.

"Hey, don't blame me," I said. "You all wanted to build it, too."

"Okay," Mama said, "don't start fighting now. That's all over. Can you think of any more memories?"

"Like the time we almost drowned out in the lake?" I asked.

"Yes, and if you only think about how scared you were, that was a bad memory. But if you think about looking up and seeing us coming to get you, that's a good memory."

"You mean it all depends on what we think about?" I asked.

"Yes," Mama said, "We make lots of memories in life, but we shouldn't keep thinking about all the bad ones, we need to think about the good ones.

"You mean like the time Lassie came around." I asked. "And she stayed long enough to save us from that mean man who came to our house?"

"Yes, I'd say that was a good memory. We all have lots of memories. But your dad has a lot of really bad memories that he can't seem to get over. I want to tell you about one of them. This happened a long time ago, when your dad was little, maybe around five. He lived with his mom and dad, an older sister, and a younger brother. His mom asked the kids if they wanted to go out for ice cream. She piled the kids in her car. They were all trying to decide if they wanted chocolate, strawberry, or vanilla. But instead of pulling up at the ice cream place, she pulled up in front of a big, old,

ICE CREAM CATASTROPHE

spooky looking building."

"This isn't the ice cream place," your dad said. "When are we going to get ice cream?"

"We have to stop here first," his mom replied.

"None of the kids wanted to get out of the car, but she insisted and hustled them inside the building. An older woman came limping down the hall, straight towards them. Her gray hair was pulled back in a tight bun and she peered over the top of tiny little glasses. Your dad never forgot the scowl on her face as she looked them over, and her deep voice as she commanded, "Follow me, children."

"Go with the nice lady," their mother said, "just be good and do whatever she tells you." Their mother turned and walked away. The kids were afraid because they didn't know what was happening. Their mother never even looked back or waved. His sister and brother started sobbing. Your dad refused to cry."

"When did she go back and get them?" I asked.

"She never did go back. They found out later that she had dropped them off at an orphans home. That's where your dad spent his childhood. He never saw or heard from his mother again. He doesn't know what happened to his dad, or his brother and sister. This is one of the bad memories he can't seem to get over. He never told me what happened in the orphanage, I probably don't even want to know. He still finds it hard to talk about. And that's only part of the story. Your dad went through other horrible things in his life."

"What else happened to him?" Ronnie asked.

"Well, it's getting late," Mama said, "and you kids need to get into bed. Try and remember some of the good things that have happened to you. See how many things you can come up with and then think about them. We'll save the rest of your dad's story for another time. And to this day, because he can't get past the memory, that's why your dad will not eat ice cream."

CHAPTER 11:
BROKEN PROMISES

"You always break your promises, so promise me you will never love me."

- Unknown

"I'll never drop you off in an orphan's home. I promise," Mama said. "you kids are my whole life. I couldn't live if anything happened to any of you."

We could always count on her promises. Mama was sitting on the couch with us, like she did every night, playing games and talking. We could come up with a lot of questions and she tried her best to answer every one. We could talk about anything for hours, nothing was off limits. Daddy never allowed us to talk. "Kids should be seen and not heard," was his motto.

We were the best kids when visiting anyone's home. We'd huddle in a group on the floor and never move. We knew better. People always commented, "Lyle, you have the best bunch of kids I ever saw."

Daddy made promises to everyone, even the bill collectors who called. He wouldn't talk to them, he made Mama do his dirty work. "Just tell them I'll make a payment next week," he'd say. Even though he made good money, the bills were always past due. When Daddy didn't keep his word, our electricity got turned off. We'd sit home in the dark, while he lingered at the cozy corner on a bar stool.

DADDY NEVER CALLED ME PRINCESS

Mama got tired of arguing with the bill collectors on the phone, so if she thought it might be one of them, she wouldn't answer. That's when they started coming to the house. When they pulled in the drive we'd follow Mama outside to hide under the maple trees until they left.

Daddy only gave Mama $20 a week for groceries. But even with that little bit of money, Mama managed to feed her family. She always had supper waiting on the table when we came home from school. Sometimes it wasn't much, maybe only plain macaroni, but she always told us: "It doesn't matter what you eat, after it's in your stomach, you're still full."

And I never realized, until years later, how carefully she must have shopped, just so she'd have a bit left after she paid for the food. I felt special because she always gave the change to me, for whatever I wanted. I wasn't doing much talking that night. I was doing a lot of thinking. Sometimes I felt like my brain was going to explode if I didn't sort everything out.

But the other kids knew that the longer they talked, the later they got to stay up. They were trying their best to keep Mama talking, but I guess she caught on.

"Okay, kids," she said, "that's enough talking for one night, it's time for bed."

Daddy didn't even wake us up one with one of his drunken rages. We slept so late we almost missed the bus. We had to run down the hill before the bus driver pulled away.

I was eager to get to school. My friend, Darcy, had been to the circus and she promised to tell me about her trip. I knew it was too much to hope that our family could go, but I enjoyed listening to her. She was so excited, telling me about all the fun she had with her family. Her grandpa even went along. She told me about all the animals, the clowns, and people on the flying trapeze.

"Men walk around selling pop, hot dogs, and best of all," she said, "big puffs of candy that looks like cotton on a stick. When you pull off a bite and put it in your mouth it disappears."

I daydreamed about cotton candy at school, and again on the long, loud, bumpy ride home. The bus let us off at the bottom of the hill and we walked the rest of the way. I was glad because I didn't want anyone to see where we really lived. We'd run for home, especially on grocery shopping day, hoping Mama would have goodies for us. We'd enjoy a snack while eagerly telling her about our day.

Mama did have a surprise when we got home, it wasn't the usual goodie, it was so much better. Daddy was going to take us to the circus on Saturday. We'd have a real family outing, just like Darcy talked about. I could hardly wait.

The only thing that might come between us and the circus was Daddy's Ham Radio. Whenever he signed on and we heard his call letters, we knew he'd disappear behind the curtain, for hours. But Daddy promised he wouldn't even sign in on the day of the circus.

Come Saturday morning we were all dressed and ready, waiting for Daddy to get up. We had to be quiet so we wouldn't wake him too soon. We were eager to go when he finally got out of bed.

"Don't be in such a hurry," he said, "I just want to check in on the Ham Radio for a couple of minutes." Then he disappeared. We all feared what that meant.

"This is KN8CWM, Charley, William, Mary. Come in, come in, come in."

"Well," Mama whispered, "we may as well find something to do to pass the time. We need to be quiet so we won't disturb him. Maybe he won't talk too long."

Mama grabbed her wish book and started looking dreamily at furniture. She was hopeful that Daddy would keep his promise to buy her a new couch. She said he could afford it, especially if he'd do without a few beers.

"Hey, Reta," Daddy yelled. "I got someone on here from Japan!

DADDY NEVER CALLED ME PRINCESS

Bring me up a beer."

Mama threw her wish book down. "Well," she said, "I guess I can stop dreaming. Your dad's more concerned about getting his next beer than he is with keeping his promise to you kids. You'll be lucky if you make it to the circus. I can probably kiss that new couch good-bye."

Us kids took turns jumping up every time he hollered for another cold one.

We were more disappointed with every hour that passed. We waited... and waited...We heard Daddy talking and laughing. We heard his calls for beer. The only thing we didn't hear was him signing off the Ham Radio. Daddy kept talking. We didn't make it to the circus. Daddy talked so long that the circus auditorium would have been empty, just like Daddy's promises.

CHAPTER 12:

MAMA'S DREAMS

"Keep your heart open to dreams. For as long as there's a dream, there is hope, and as long as there is hope, there is joy in living."

- Anonymous

"Mama, what are you doing with Daddy's hand saw?"

Mama was a spur of the moment type of person. Nothing surprised me with the unusual things she did. She made life interesting, most of the time. But that day she was scaring me. The look on her face was spooky. Her eyes were all big and mean looking. Her red hair looked more frizzy and wilder that usual. Her lips were pursed tightly together.

"I'm tired of all this old second-hand stuff," Mama yelled. "especially this ugly old gray couch. I've had it, I can't stand to look at it another day. Your dad promised to buy me some new furniture. Yeah, right! Dream on! He can't turn any of his precious money loose. He might miss a couple of beers, or low and behold, maybe even a few steaks."

Mama was embarrassed when anyone came over. She'd admire other people's furniture when we went visiting. She especially liked a couch that came in two separate pieces, called a sectional, because it could be arranged in a number of ways.

An old, worn-thin and tattered sheet covered our couch. Mama ripped the cover right off. She jumped up in the middle of the sofa

DADDY NEVER CALLED ME PRINCESS

and planted her feet in the cushions. She raised the hand saw up in the air then lowered it down on top of the old couch. She started sawing. The fabric ripped. Guts started falling out all over the cement floor. Before long the sawdust was flying. I watched in horror, knowing that Daddy was going to kill her when he came home.

"Mama, why are you cutting our couch?"

"I'm going to make me a sectional."

Mama was huffing and puffing and wiping sweat from her face. But she kept at it until the old couch was in two separate pieces. Mama scooped up the stuffing that had fallen out and shoved it back inside the couch. She made a few trips outside and carried in four cement blocks, then arranged the two separate pieces of the couch until they satisfied her. One cement block went under each corner. She found a couple of better sheets that weren't so thread bare. With a smile on her face she covered each piece.

And Wham-O, Mama had her sectional.

She spent the rest of the afternoon proudly rearranging the other meager pieces of furniture. I lived in fear of what Daddy would do to her when he came home. I was hoping that he'd just head to the cozy corner bar after work, as usual, and that it wouldn't be one of those rare occasions where he came straight home. But no such luck, he came straight home.

He walked in the house, but at least he was sober. He noticed the two pieces of furniture, one on each side of his overstuffed chair.

"Well what in the world did you do now?" He asked Mama.

"Well, you wouldn't buy me a sectional," she said. "So I made my own."

Daddy just grinned and shook his head. He must have felt guilty because he told Mama he'd take her shopping, just to look, if she could get a baby sitter. She didn't waste any time calling someone.

MAMA'S DREAMS

"Strike while the iron's hot," she whispered to me, "and he just got paid."

The next day Mama told us all about their shopping trip. Daddy didn't buy her the sectional she wanted, but he did end up buying her a brand new recliner. The chair was a soft maroon color, with an extra thick cushion, just like the one in her wish book. But we never did get to see for ourselves. Daddy had the chair in the back of his open pick-up truck. He stopped at the bar on the way home so he and Mama could run in for a quick one. When they came out, the chair was gone.

Mama's one new piece of furniture, but she never even got to bring the chair home.

Daddy was in a bad mood after that, even more so than usual. Someone pulled in the end of our long drive, just so they could turn around. Daddy saw them and grabbed his rifle. He ran down the driveway pointing the gun at them, cussing and screaming.

"Get out of here, you no-good scum. Nobody turns around in my driveway."

"Lyle, they're going to call the cops on you," Mama said.

"Well, I don't care," he said as he came back in the house and laid his weapon on the table, "this is my house and I don't want anyone trespassing while I'm here."

Later that day, some people from church came to our door selling Bibles. Daddy grabbed his rifle and ran them off, too. "God bless you, sir," they cried, as they scrambled to their car, tripping over their own feet.

"Well, I guess I took care of them," Daddy laughed. "They won't come back."

He grabbed his jacket, headed out the door, jumped in his car and took off. We all knew where he'd end up, at least until the bar's last call. Mama said people at the bar all acted like they thought Daddy was a great guy. No one knew what he was really like at

DADDY NEVER CALLED ME PRINCESS

home. Mama kept her bruises well hidden; emotional scars don't show and we all had plenty of them.

That night when he came home Mama got up to cook the steak he'd bought. I could hear them talking.

"Guess who I ran into tonight?"

"Who?"

"Oh, you're just never gonna guess..."

"Well tell me, don't keep me in suspense."

"Just hold your horses, I'm getting to it. I'll tell you. There was a man sitting at the bar talking. When the bar tender called him by name I almost fell over: we both had the same full name. I wondered if it was even possible, after all these years of not even knowing if he was dead or alive. But I found out that it was him. The man sitting beside me was my dad!"

"You're kidding! I might have known that if you ran into each other it would be in a bar."

"What a better place," Daddy laughed. "He was passing through town and just stopped at the bar for a cold one. We downed a few beers together and talked for hours. He's only living about 300 miles from here. He has a house in Oscoda. How would you like that dream house you're always talking about?"

"I'd love a new house," Mama said, "but how are you going to manage that?"

"I found out that my dad's a licensed carpenter. He agreed to move in with us and then we could build the place together. You'd have that real house you've always wanted, with a big kitchen to do all your baking in. You wouldn't have to carry water anymore. We'd have indoor plumbing with a bathtub. No more pot to carry and dump. You could have a house that you'd be proud of."

I heard the excitement in Mama's voice. Maybe her dream was about to become true. "Could you put in a basement," she said, "so

MAMA'S DREAMS

we'd have someplace to go during tornadoes?"

"Yes, we could even put in a basement."

"I'd love it," she said, "when can you start?"

"I'll run up north this weekend and talk to my dad again. He has to tie up loose ends there first. The sooner he's able to do that, the sooner we can start drawing up the blueprints."

"If he comes to live with us," Mama said, "I'll have to shove that sectional back together so your dad will have someplace to sleep. Things would sure be crowded around here. But I could certainly manage, if we'd get a new house out of the deal."

Finding out that we had a grandpa on Daddy's side, and that he was going to come and live with us, brought many different feelings. Would he be one of those grandpas that we could love and feel safe with, like Darcy's grandpa? Or would he be just another drinking buddy for Daddy, just another guy who loved the bottle more, just another man we'd have to keep away from?

I was hoping he'd be a nice grandpa.

I could hardly wait to go to school the next day so I could talk to my best friend, Darcy. I had so much to tell her. I was going over all of it in my mind. We have a grandpa, and he's going to come and live with us. Him and Daddy are going to build a new house. I'm going to get my own bedroom so maybe you can come and spend the night. We'll plan a lot of fun things to do together...

Mama had been cutting pictures out of magazines for as long as I could remember. Pictures of a brick house, with a view through the big picture window. Pictures of a nice kitchen, with lots of oak cupboards. And a bathroom with running water, a real bathtub, and a big mirror. Mama would be so happy. She deserved to have some comfort and pleasure in her life. Dreams can come true, sometimes, and I was so hoping that Mama's would.

I enjoyed lying in bed that night, listening to something besides fighting for a change. No screaming, only excited voices. The

DADDY NEVER CALLED ME PRINCESS

nighttime crickets even sounded happy. Just before I drifted off to sleep I could hear Mama telling Daddy about all the things she wanted to have in the house of her dreams.

"And a large, old-fashioned, real brick fireplace…"

CHAPTER 13:

INVISIBLE

"Everyone has an invisible sign hanging from their neck saying, 'Make me feel important.'
Never forget this message when working with people."

— Mary Kay Ash

"Where did everyone go?"

I wanted to tell Darcy my good news, but I walked into my fourth grade class only to be welcomed by a bunch of empty chairs. My teacher had changed rooms and I didn't know anything about the switch. Standing in the middle of that quiet room I felt abandoned and invisible. The teacher had probably sent a note home, but I wasn't there to get a copy. All of us kids missed a lot of school. Either we didn't have anything for lunch, or we didn't have any shoes to wear, or occasionally we were sick. Sometimes Mama needed help with the other kids, or maybe she just wanted someone to stay home with her. I could count on one hand the full weeks of school I attended, without missing at least one day. But I always had a written excuse from Mama, so what could they do?

One of my teachers told me, "You're smart, you could be a straight A student, if you'd just come to school all the time." But I never had the chance to find out.

Standing in that empty classroom made me feel so scared and alone. I was too afraid to ask anyone where my class went. I walked to the principals' office and told her I was sick and needed to go

DADDY NEVER CALLED ME PRINCESS

home. Someone from the office drove me home.

"Just drop me off at the bottom of the hill," I told him, "the bus driver does and I'll walk from there."

"Well you won't have to walk today," he said, "not in this cold weather."

I was so embarrassed when he insisted on taking me all the way home. I didn't want him to see where we really lived. I wished our house had been invisible.

But Mama was glad when I came home early and we had fun together. We watched Queen for a Day. The host, Jack Bailey, would come on and shout.

"Do YOU want to be Queen for a Day!?"

Then four women, each with a sob story, told why they believed they should be crowned "Queen." They awarded prizes like a washer and dryer. I knew that if Mama got on the show she'd win. Then she wouldn't have to wash in that old wringer washer and hang them outside to dry, even in cold weather. All the clothes were stiff as a board when she brought them in.

Ronnie looked froze when he came in from school. Mama brushed the snow off and fixed him some hot cocoa. We had supper and played games til bedtime. Our only heat was a stove in the middle of the room and we were cold. Mama told us to get into bed. She ironed the sheets, then, one at a time, ran real fast and wrapped one of the heated sheets around each of us. With blankets or coats piled on top, we were cozy and warm. We fell asleep, til Daddy came home.

No matter how hard we slept, our dreams would be interrupted by headlights shining in the bedroom window, or the sound of his keys, and fear gripped our hearts. Daddy would stumble in the door and bark his orders at Mama.

"Hey, woman, get out of that bed and cook me a steak."

Before long, the smell of his nightly T-bone or porterhouse

wafted through the rooms. If fighting started, things would escalate rapidly. Daddy would take his frustrations out on Mama with his fists. Mama used her mouth. I remember lying in bed, shaking, and I always prayed the same prayer.

"Please, Jesus, make Mama shut up!"

That's the trouble with Mama. She was too in Daddy's face, visible. Nothing ever excused him from beating her. Still, she always egged him on.

"Does that make you feel like a man?" she'd yell, "Well, go ahead then, hit me again."

And Daddy always obliged.

"Okay, you hit me on this side," she'd say, "now why not try for the other side?"

And BAM, he'd hit her again. I was afraid he was going to break her neck. I never knew what would happen. Would Daddy take a break, and be still long enough to pass out? Would I hear Daddy snoring and Mama going back to bed? Or would Mama come after me because Daddy had kicked us out, again. I knew I was on the way out if I heard the word "illegitimate."

I laid in bed listening and remembering all the times I wished Trixie was an attack dog. Especially when Daddy started beating on Mama, then Trixie could protect her. But all chances of that happening had ended a few weeks earlier. Mama sent me over to borrow something from one of the neighbor's. I was carrying Trixie in my arms. Their daughter, who was a little older than me, answered the door. She said something to me and I thought she was being a smart aleck. I guess Trixie thought the same thing, because she growled at the girl, then leaned over and bit her right on the lip. The girl touched her bloody lip, then started screaming and ran for her mom. After the neighbor told Daddy what happened, he said he'd take care of it and she didn't have to worry about it ever happening again. Daddy took my beloved dog away in a pillowcase and I never even got to say good-bye.

DADDY NEVER CALLED ME PRINCESS

But as I listened, everything turned quiet. I heard Daddy snoring and Mama went back to bed. Everything was okay for the rest of the night.

I dreamed about the all the fun I was hoping to have the next day.

The school was taking us on a field trip to the Shrine Circus. My class boarded the bus and we were on the way. I was looking forward to the trip, since Daddy never did take our family. Cotton candy was something I'd only heard about from Darcy and it sounded good.

The circus was held at the IMA, a huge arena. The place was packed when our bus pulled in. My class followed the teacher and suddenly we were in a different world. Everything about the circus was spectacular, from the round stadium, to the rows and rows of seats all around the inside. Our teacher led us to seats way up high in the bleachers. There were funny looking clowns with big red noses, painted faces, and clothes that were much too big for them. Most people laughed at the clowns, a few little kids cried because they were scared, but not me. I had fun. We watched the elephants parade around the ring in rhinestone collars. Pretty ladies rode horses that were all decked out in fancy outfits. There were lion tamers, tigers and also jugglers. My favorite was the people on the flying trapeze, even if they did cause me to hold my breath for fear that they were going to fall and miss the net.

People were buying hot dogs and pop, but I didn't have any money. When a man walked by holding up fluffy clouds of pink and blue heaven on a stick, I almost drooled. I was so enticed by the man and no one noticed, not even my teacher, when I followed him. I kept walking behind the man and watching the kids as their mouths turned pink and blue from the cotton candy. Suddenly I looked around and I didn't know where I was. I tried to find my class but there were too many people. The circus was over and the place started clearing out. My class had left without me. I felt so scared and alone, wondering why no one even noticed that I was gone. But, then again, I shouldn't have been surprised, I always felt

INVISIBLE

like no one ever really saw me anyway.

Like the time Mama made me so mad I told her I hated her and I was going to run away.

"Well, here," Mama said, "I'll help you pack."

She probably thought she was helping, but she only made me feel worse. I didn't go far. I just ran out beside the road, looked for the deepest ditch, and climbed in. I laid down using the little bag I'd packed for a pillow. Dogs barked and cars whizzed by, but no one even noticed I was there. I felt invisible.

Just about dark I crawled out of the ditch and walked slowly back to the house.

"Well, I knew you'd be back," Mama said, "as soon as you got hungry enough."

I'd been standing at the circus for a long time, hoping someone would come looking for me, but no one came, and I was starving. I finally gathered up enough courage to walk over to a friendly looking lady. I told her I was lost. She called the police. They came and took me home. My teacher never missed me, or even called to see if I got home safely. And I never got a hot dog, or a drink, and worst of all, no cotton candy.

Daddy never seemed to lack for food or drink. He lived on steak and booze. Back at home Ronnie was behind the curtain, which was off limits, snooping around in Daddy's stuff.

"Hey, Mama," he yelled, "come and see what I found in Daddy's desk."

Mama went in there and found cheese, crackers, packages of Beef Jerky, cans of sardines, and other dried treats. "Well, that rotten drunk!" she said. "Come on kids, let's have a party."

And we did. Mama loaded up all the treats and took them into the kitchen. She poured us each a glass of Kool Aid. We tore open all the wrappers and had a ball eating. Except Mama was the only one who liked the sardines. "Won't Daddy be mad when he finds

DADDY NEVER CALLED ME PRINCESS

out?" I asked.

"Well, the nerve of him, hiding a secret stash of food while we're starving. He better not say one word. But I'd love to see the look on his face when he pulls out his drawer, especially if he comes home drunk. I wonder what he'll do when he looks for all his hidden goodies, and finds out that everything has vanished."

CHAPTER 14:
UNDERCOVER BABYSITTERS

"It's important to talk about it. You raise awareness. But you can also prevent it
(child abuse) by not letting it be a secret."

- Shari Pulliam

The sixteen year old babysitter's name was Molly. She had watched us before. I didn't have to be afraid of her, or so I thought. Mama wouldn't let me babysit, I was only ten.

Molly put Ronnie, Penny, and the baby to bed. Since I was the oldest, I got to stay up later. She asked me if I wanted to play cards. I didn't know how, but she said she'd teach me. She shuffled. When I looked at my cards I couldn't believe my eyes. There were pictures of men and women, doing very strange things, totally naked.

"Here, Wanda," Molly said, "Pick one of my cards and do things like that to me."

I knew it wasn't right, so I said, "No, I'm not going to do that."

Molly grabbed my hands and tried to force me to touch her in private places. I pulled away. All the cards went flying. I ran and started to climb out the nearest open window. Molly grabbed me by my hair before I even hit the ground. She wouldn't turn loose. I tried with all my strength to get away, and it felt like she tried with all her power to keep me there. My head was hurting so bad, but I was not going to go back in that house with her. I thought she was

DADDY NEVER CALLED ME PRINCESS

going to pull every hair right out of my head. She'd pull and force me a little ways back in the window and I'd pull and get a little ways back outside. Finally, with the last ounce of strength I had, one final jerk landed me on the ground. I ran off and hid outside. How, or when, I got back in the house, I can't say. My next memory was telling Mama what Molly did to me.

"I'll talk to her," Mama said, "but she's a girl, at least she can't rape you."

I knew Grandpa was moving in soon; maybe he could be our babysitter then.

I was nervous and needed some candy. Ronnie, Penny, and I gathered up a load of empty bottles. We had quite a stash and the bag was spilling over. Bottles kept falling out. I'd pick them up and try to carry the extras in my arms. Suddenly I tripped and fell. Broken bottles cut me and blood poured down my arms and legs.

"Mama, Wanda cut herself," Penny yelled, "she's bleeding all over the place."

Mama ran out, took one look at me, then went in and grabbed a couple of old towels to wrap around my blood soaked arms. "Ronnie, and Penny, you stay with Rodney," she said.

Mama rushed me across the road. "Well those cuts are pretty deep," the neighbor said, "I think she's going to need stitches."

"I don't have money for a doctor," Mama said, "I don't have a car, and I can't even drive."

So Mama and the neighbor just put pressure on the cuts until the bleeding stopped. They cleaned and bandaged me up as best they knew how and called it good.

My sore arms got me out of school for a few extra days. Mama took real good care of me. She fixed my food and served it on a tray with a little red flower. She let me watch whatever I wanted on television. I liked Father Knows Best. I always wished I had a Daddy like that, someone who would love me and call me his little

UNDERCOVER BABYSITTERS

"Princess." Daddy, at his best, only called me "Hey, Wanda," but it was never for anything good.

When my arms healed I went back to school. Daddy was going to take Mama dancing. We needed a babysitter. I begged Mama not to get Molly. One of our neighbor's told Mama that her baby brother watched her kids all the time and he was real good, so Mama asked him. He agreed to watch us, but only if he could watch us over at his sisters house, just down the road a bit. So Mama bundled us all up that Saturday. We walked over to his sisters house. Her brother was there waiting for us when Mama dropped us off.

There was something about him that I didn't like, but I wasn't sure what. We all played games, the kids were laughing with him, until bedtime. He put the other kids to bed.

"You're older," he told me, "so you can stay up longer."

He wanted to watch television on the couch. He wanted me to sit beside him. I tried to keep down on one end, but he kept scooting over closer to me.

"You're so pretty," he said, "you must have lots of boys after you."

"No," I told him, "I'm not old enough to have a boyfriend, and Daddy wouldn't let me."

"What he doesn't know, won't hurt him. I can be your boyfriend. We don't have to tell."

He started putting his hands underneath my dress. I tried to push him away, but he was so strong. I grabbed the lamp off the table and tried to hit him over the head with it. We wrestled. He smacked me in the face and my nose started bleeding. Somehow, I was able to pull away. I ran into the bathroom and locked the door. I was worried about the other kids, asleep in bed. I wondered if I should go back out for them, but I listened at the door and didn't hear any noise. So I found an old washrag and held it on my nose until the bleeding stopped, then I cleaned the blood off my face and clothes. I just sat on the floor crying, and I wouldn't open the

DADDY NEVER CALLED ME PRINCESS

door.

"Come on out," he said, "I won't touch you anymore. Let's just watch television."

But I wouldn't come out, no matter how much he tried to coax me. I stayed there until Mama came. She saw the blood and wasn't too surprised. I had nosebleeds quite often.

"Another bloody nose?" was all she said. The next day I told her about everything that had happened.

"Well, that filthy kid, I guess he won't be babysitting for you again."

He must have been afraid that I was going to tell on him. He was gone the next day. I didn't even know where he lived.

Mama went through many different babysitters over the years. All of them tried something, at least once, in one form or another. One of them even tried to smother me with a pillow, when I told her I was going to tell.

I couldn't wait until our grandpa came. I wouldn't have to worry about the long list of strange babysitters anymore. Wouldn't we surely be safe with our grandpa?

CHAPTER 15:
GRANDPA

"Love is unconditional, relationships are not."

- Grant Gudmundson

    The big day finally arrived. We would meet our grandpa for the first time. Mama cleaned and polished our old furniture til everything shined. Then she kept herself busy by walking around, picking up small pieces of lint off the floor. Mama didn't like new people coming around, they made her nervous. Sometimes, I didn't think she liked people at all. Most of them anyway. I think she was just embarrassed about our house and she lived in fear that Daddy would come home unexpectedly and do something to hurt their feelings. Mama said he came home at those time just to catch us doing something. But she didn't have to worry about much company, Daddy took care of that, no one wanted to come around him.

    I remember one time when Uncle Pete came over. He was my favorite Uncle. He was such a wonderful person that he was everyone's favorite. I never heard him say a bad word about anyone and he never swore or even raised his voice. He was always smiling and happy. He brought some ice cream that day, so he could help Mama celebrate her birthday.

    Uncle Pete gave everyone a hug and we all hugged him back. Mama got out some bowls to dish up the ice cream that was sitting on the counter when we heard a car pull in the drive.

DADDY NEVER CALLED ME PRINCESS

Our fun was over, it was Daddy.

He came storming in the house, drunk as usual, and looked at Uncle Pete.

"And what brings you over to our neck of the woods? I thought you were too good to come around the likes of us." He said.

"Oh, I just thought I'd bring some ice cream as a little treat for everyone."

"Well we don't need your stupid ice cream. And we don't need you coming around here bringing treats. Here's what you can do with your blasted ice cream!"

Daddy picked up the carton of ice cream and slammed it against the wall.

"That's what I think of your ice cream."

The carton ripped and ice cream splattered all over the kitchen. Mama was so embarrassed. The words Daddy used I wouldn't repeat, but he ordered Uncle Pete to get out.

Mama started to argue with him but Uncle Pete told her it was alright.

Mama grabbed a rag and bent down to clean up the mess. Uncle Pete knelt down beside her. "It's Okay, Reta," he whispered. "I'm leaving now."

That's the last we saw of my favorite uncle for a long time. Mama said Daddy was just jealous of him because Uncle Pete was such a nice guy and he knew how much we all liked him.

The only ones who did come around were Daddy's drinking buddy's, and we could have done without all of them. I wondered how it would be when Grandpa got here.

The sound of every car that came down that dirt road sent us all running to the window. Daddy pulled in the drive that Saturday with Grandpa right behind him, bag and baggage.

"Hey, Reta," he told Mama, "this is my dad."

GRANDPA

"Nice to meet you," she said. She tried to shake his hand, but he hugged her instead.

"Hey, Lyle," he told Daddy. "You sure got you a looker there."

"Hey, kids," Mama said. "Come and meet your grandpa."

"What a nice family you have here. You should be so proud. Now you kids come over here. Give your old grandpa a hug."

He didn't look a lot like Daddy. Grandpa was a lot heavier, and much shorter. His hair wasn't red, and what he did have was all gray. Big round glasses covered most of his face and he kept pushing them up. A big checkered flannel shirt hung over baggy jeans. But he had a gentle looking face. Mama had supper ready so we all sat down together.

Grandpa and Daddy talked about what they'd been doing since they were separated. He found out where his brother and sister lived and how they were getting along. But none of them knew what happened to their mother, or if she was even still alive. They talked long into the night as the beer bottles piled up, the ashtrays overflowed, and the smoke never cleared.

Time passed, Grandpa seemed to fit into our world, even though I heard Daddy say that his dad was impulsive & ornery. Mama asked Daddy if he thought some of that had rubbed off on him. Daddy and Grandpa drew up plans for our new house. First they dug the basement. Then they started hauling materials home, and, little by little, we watched our house take shape.

 Grandpa did baby sit, and we all had fun together. He liked to have us sit around him while he read stories. Things were going along pretty well, except Grandpa liked to drink, too. Sometimes, while they worked on the house, Daddy and Grandpa would get in big fights. But they always managed to settle their differences, then they'd get back to working.

Grandpa seemed to like Mama, a lot. He was always always talking to her and saying sexy things when Daddy was gone. "Oh, he only talks like that when he's drunk," Mama said, "but he wouldn't

DADDY NEVER CALLED ME PRINCESS

ever bother you kids."

I asked Mama if she told Daddy how Grandpa acted around her when he was gone.

"Are you kidding?" she said. "Your dad would kill him, so don't you dare say anything."

I was worried about Mama, but she didn't seem to be afraid, and I figured since he only liked older women, then Penny and I were safe. Maybe he just liked to hang around Mama because she was such a great cook. Everyone said so. She could make the best pies in the whole world. Lemon meringue, strawberry, banana, whatever she had on hand. She always made her own crust! Her pies were so flaky and delicious.

"Hey, Wanda," Mama said. "Go pick some raspberries and I'll make a pie for supper."

Grabbing a pail, I went out back to pick berries. Looking up, I saw Grandpa coming, swinging a pail, too. On no! I felt like running. I hope he's coming after berries.

"Nice day out today," he said. "I thought I'd come and help you pick berries."

"That's okay," I told him, "I can get them by myself. I do it all the time."

But Grandpa started picking berries and putting them in his pail.

"You're growing up into an a pretty little thing. Do you have a boyfriend?"

"No, I'm not old enough yet. I'm only eleven."

"Well, it won't be long. You're going to have to learn how to please a man. I can teach you everything you need to know, so you'll be ready. Let me show you how to diddle."

I took off running toward the house.

"Now, don't tell your dad about this." he yelled. "I didn't even

GRANDPA

touch you. I was just trying to help you."

I told Mama. "That dirty old man," she said. "Just keep away from him from now on. The next time he wants to teach you how to diddle, tell him, I don't know what that is, but I'll go ask Mama if you can show me."

Another time while I was sitting under the maple tree, reading, Grandpa came out.

"Well, that's looks like a nice relaxing thing to be doing on such a beautiful day. I can show you how to relax even more. I can teach you how to diddle."

"I don't know what that is," I said, "but I'll ask Mama if you can show me."

"No," he said, as he took off his hat and wiped the sweat off his face. "You better not ask her, she wouldn't understand what you need."

But Mama's words never stopped him. He just started in with other nasty remarks. Or he'd try to grab me in ways that I knew weren't right. He was hard to ignore.

The next time Daddy took Mama out dancing, they still had Grandpa babysit.

I couldn't keep away from him, like Mama told me, but when he went over to check on something next door, I locked him out of the house. He came and beat on the door. I wouldn't let him in. Penny peeked out the curtains, then ran, and before I could grab her, she had her hand on the door knob.

"No! I yelled, "Don't open the door."

"Why can't I open the door?" she asked. "It's Grandpa."

How could I explain things to Penny? She was only six years old.

"Just believe me," I told her. Grandpa's not very nice and he tries to do bad things."

DADDY NEVER CALLED ME PRINCESS

But she didn't believe me. She liked Grandpa. Whenever he was around and we were alone with him, I knew I'd have to keep my eye out for Penny, too.

We heard a car start up and ran to the window. Grandpa's car was pulling out the driveway. We didn't relax for too long because he came back. He must have ran up to the store for another six pack. But he didn't try to get in, he just went next door and left us alone.

I put Penny and the others to bed and sat up for while, peeking out the windows, until I could barely hold my eyes open. Then I went to bed. Hours later I woke up when I heard Mama and Daddy laughing and talking. I was glad she had a good time dancing. But I was tired of being scared at home. As much as I tried, it was hard to 'Just keep away from him,' like Mama told me. Penny was too young to understand, so I had to keep a close watch on her, too. I worried about it all the time—candy didn't even help. Something had to give.

CHAPTER 16:
SCARED TO BREATHE

"To him who is in fear, everything rustles."

- Sophocles

Grandpa couldn't be trusted, so I did like Mama told me, and I tried to keep away from him. My sister, Penny, was in second grade then, and I tried to keep a close watch on her.

Work on our new house continued, at least it did between Daddy and Grandpa's fights. Grandpa gave the orders because, as a licensed carpenter, he thought he knew best. Grandpa got "so" mad, when his orders weren't followed, and he'd take off. After a few days, he'd come back and we'd hear table saws and hammers again.

Daddy would get mad because he didn't like anyone telling him what to do, he liked giving orders. Grandpa wouldn't follow his orders so Daddy took his frustrations out on Ronnie.

One of his chores was to bring in the paper every day. Once in a while, he'd forget. No matter what time Daddy came home, if his paper wasn't sitting beside his chair, he'd have a fit.

"Hey, Ronnie!" He'd yell while dragging him out of bed. "You didn't bring my paper in today. Now get up, go outside and get it!"

"But it's dark out there, I can't see."

Daddy would shove him outside, slam the door, then stagger

DADDY NEVER CALLED ME PRINCESS

over to lean out the window. "You walk out there and get that paper, and you're not getting back in this house until you do!"

Ronnie would inch his way out to the road, screaming with every step. After what seemed like forever, he'd come back with the precious paper.

"Well, it's about time," Daddy would bark. "Now maybe you won't forget it next time."

But, more often than not, he'd still forget to bring in the paper, probably out of spite.

Ronnie took his anger out by scaring everyone else. He'd hide under our bed at night, then he'd sneak his hand up, yell something spooky and grab us. Or he'd hide around the corner, then scream and jump out when we walked by. Or he'd hook fishing line to Mama's purse, when no one was looking. Then, with everyone sitting quietly watching television, he'd hide and pull her bag using the fishing line. Her purse would seem to walk across the floor on its own.

But Ronnie wasn't the only one who scared us. Coming home from school I saw Penny running up the road yelling at me. "Something's wrong with Mama, come quick."

With my heart in my throat, I ran up the hill towards home. Ronnie was right behind me. I burst in the door to see Mama lying on the floor, flat on her back. Her arms were folded across her chest, like she was in a casket. She was surrounded by silk flowers. The minute I saw her I realized she was only pretending to be dead. I was furious! I threw all my books on the floor and cried. "Well, that was a dirty rotten trick to play on us!"

Mama jumped up. "Well I'm sorry, I thought you'd know I was only playing. I just wanted to see how much you two loved me and find out who would run the fastest."

I ran fast after that, right into my bedroom. My little bag of candy was always within reach. I'd write poems and stories, and read anything I could get my hands on, even the set of encyclopedias that Daddy bought from a friend.

Modern Romances was something else I liked. I could transport my life to one of being in love and feeling special to a boy. But in reality, I was so afraid of men, that if a boy even looked at me, I'd run the other way. Boys only wanted one thing, and I didn't trust any of them.

Once a week we'd watch, "The Adventures of Ozzie and Harriet." Ricky Nelson was my idol. At the end of every show, he'd grab his guitar and sing one of his songs. I just lived for those nights. A lot of the girls liked Elvis, and I did too, but Ricky was my favorite. My eyes would be glued to the television when he sang, "Have I Told You Lately That I Love You," or "Honeycomb," or anything else. I'd watch television, and dream, as a way to escape.

One of Mama's favorite programs was "Wagon Train," and her favorite actor was the dashing scout, Robert Horton. He always rode ahead of the wagon train, scouting for the bad guys, then he'd ride back and warn everyone. I pulled a trick on Mama. I came home from school, rushed in the house and told her that Robert Horton was riding up the road on his horse. I must have been very convincing, because she rushed out to look for her non-existent dream man.

Mama's favorite dream was living in a real house, and hers was finally coming together. The outside was finished and they were working on the inside. Two bedrooms were upstairs. Ronnie and Rodney would have their own bedroom, and Penny and I would share a bedroom. Then we wouldn't have to worry about Ronnie hiding under the bed and scaring us. But all of our dreams came to an abrupt halt.

Daddy and Grandpa had a huge fight about the fireplace, the worst ever. Grandpa got mad and took off. We all waited for him to come back, but that time he never did. Mama answered the telephone and was shocked and saddened by what she heard. Grandpa had been sitting on a bar stool, drinking, when he had a heart attack. Grandpa never walked away from that bar stool. He

DADDY NEVER CALLED ME PRINCESS

died on the spot. I'm sure Daddy's heart was broken, but, if so, he wasn't about to let any of us know how he felt. All work on our house stopped. We heard predictions that we were in for a bad winter, so Daddy decided to move us into our new house, even though it wasn't finished and looked kind of scary.

An old coal stove provided heat. We wouldn't be using the upstairs so a 4×8 sheet of plywood covered the hole. We didn't get our own bedrooms, we still shared. There were no walls and we still had to make do without indoor plumbing. All the floors were plywood sub floors.

The last box had been carried over and at least we were out of the little garage we had called home for so long. Daddy ran back to the bar.

We all climbed into bed for the first night in our new place. We were awakened by spooky noises in the dark. The eerie sounds continued and sent all of us running scared, straight into bed with Mama. "What was that?" we all asked.

"Well," she said, "sometimes a noise is just the house settling... and sometimes not."

CHAPTER 17:
WATCH THE FLAMES

"So, like a forgotten fire, a childhood can always flare up again within us."

- Gaston Bachelard

Daddy caught us playing with fire.

We were just trying to have fun by building our own fire pit. He never let us forget that night, as if we ever could. We all got our first spanking, then lived in fear that he was going to beat us, like he did our Mother. But he didn't beat us all physically. He only terrified us with the insane things he did. The incident happened three years earlier and he still brought it up.

"So you kids like fire?" he said, "I'll show you a fire."

Daddy got up and staggered outside, then came back in rolling a big black tire. He lifted the heavy tire, threw it in the fireplace, then squirted on some lighter fluid. Flames shot clear out into the room. We all jumped back. The whole house started to rumble and vibrate, like the roar of a tornado. Black smoke rolled out, filled up the room and burned our eyes. Our clothes and bodies turned black. The fact that the house didn't catch on fire was a miracle. Daddy just laughed. He thought scaring us was hilarious. When everything finally died down the entire house was covered in black soot. Mama had a horrid mess to clean up, and the smell lingered on.

DADDY NEVER CALLED ME PRINCESS

Even the next morning, when we got on the school bus, kids asked why we smelled like smoke. When we came home from school there were fire trucks in our yard and I wondered what Daddy had done. But our mother was outside talking to one of the firemen and I found out it hadn't been Daddy, it was her.

"Ma'am, it's too windy today, you shouldn't have tried to burn anything."

"Well," Mama said, "I thought everything would be okay in the burning barrel."

But everything hadn't been okay, she'd set the woods on fire. Thankfully, the fireman had managed to get there in time to put the fire out before it spread too far. Being close to all those fires had been pretty scary. But that was nothing compared to what else we had to witness.

Mama had spent a lot of time cleaning up the smoke damage. Daddy promised to take her dancing, to make up for all the hard work he'd caused. I tried to convince her to let me baby sit, since I was twelve years old by then. She would agree to anything, if I kept asking enough times. Besides, I was tired of worrying about who was going to watch us. After giving me all the usual warnings of don't let them play with matches, don't answer the door to strangers, don't eat everything in the house, she finally agreed. "Now you kids do what Wanda tells you to," she said. "I've spent all day cleaning this house, and you better keep it that way while I'm gone."

We watched her get ready for the big night. After her bath I smelled Tabu dusting powder. Her green dress had lots of tiny pleats and was covered in sparkling sequins. She never had to curl her hair, she just washed it and the curls behaved. The most she ever had to do was take her finger, spit on it, wrap some hair around it, and twirl a couple of extra curls at the sides. She called them "Spit Curls." A long silver necklace looked pretty with matching ear rings that dangled beneath her red curls. Her black high heels had open toes. She added a few squirts of Tabu cologne

WATCH THE FLAMES

for the finishing touch, then she modeled for us.

"Wow, you look so pretty," I told her. "I can see you dancing already."

She absolutely loved to dance, especially the polka. She'd take me in her arms and dance me around as she'd sing, "Roll out the barrel, we'll have a barrel of fun." She was so looking forward to her night out.

"You're going to have so much fun. Don't worry about us, I just hope Daddy comes home in a good mood."

So she waited for Daddy, and waited, and waited. She was pacing the floor with her hands on her hips, watching out the window, and sighing a lot.

"He probably went straight to the bar after work, instead of coming home to get me. I bet he's sitting there, boozing it up with all the other drunks. Then he'll probably come home after the bars close and want me to cook him a steak. Well, if that's what he does, and I have to get up and cook a steak, then I hope he chokes to death on it."

He never came home, at least not in time to take her dancing. She finally let out a huge sigh, got up from the couch, and stomped into the bedroom. "I guess I won't need these dancing clothes tonight." She came back out, all red faced, wearing what she called her "comfy clothes." We all watched the Donna Reed show and a couple of others, then went to bed. At three in the morning, Daddy's booming voice jarred us awake.

"Hey, Reta, get out of that bed and cook me a steak."

Mama got up and I heard her bang the pan on the stove as she put his steak on to cook. Things quieted down and before long the smell of Porterhouse steak and mushrooms drifted into the bedroom. Daddy started eating. Suddenly, he made choking sounds.

"Lyle, Lyle," Mama yelled. "Are you okay?"

All of us kids were awake, we knew there would probably be a

DADDY NEVER CALLED ME PRINCESS

fight that night, so we had a hard time sleeping. We jumped out of bed and headed towards the living room. We hid around the corner and peeked at them. Daddy was holding his throat, his eyes were bugging out and he was turning blue. Mama kept screaming, but she didn't do anything.

Finally, Daddy coughed up the piece of steak he'd been choking on.

"Well that was a close one," Mama said. "You had me so scared, I couldn't move."

I knew she didn't really want him to die.

Daddy finished his steak. He was so drunk that he passed out in no time. Us kids stood in the hall, quietly. Then I couldn't believe what we watched Mama do next. Daddy had been smoking and the cigarette was still dangling from between his fingers. She gently took the cigarette out of his hands, she pulled back the cuff of his pants, and dropped the lit cigarette down in his pant cuff.

We watched in horror. What could we do, yell? "Hey, Daddy, Mama's trying to catch you on fire." He would definitely kill her. Daddy's pant leg started to smoke.

Suddenly Mama had a change of heart. She starting patting Daddy's pants to put out the fire. "Wake up Lyle," she yelled, "you're on fire, you must have dropped your cigarette down your pant legs."

Daddy jumped up, dropped his pants, and tried to get them off. But, since she refused to mend his clothes, in order to keep his torn pant cuffs up, he had wired them around his legs. He couldn't get them off, without a pair of wire cutters, so his pants just fell at his ankles. But, at least he managed to put the fire out.

"See what you get," Mama said, "coming home drunk and passing out. You could have burned the whole house down, and all of us too."

"Oh well," he laughed, "at least I didn't."

WATCH THE FLAMES

With the excitement over for the night, we all went back to bed.

The next day was Saturday. Daddy didn't have to work so he was sleeping late. Us kids were quietly watching television when someone knocked at the door. Mama opened the door and a strange man was standing there. He was wearing old torn coveralls, a plaid shirt, and dirty boots. A black cap was pulled down over his eyes.

"My car broke down," he said, "I've been walking on these dusty country roads. Could I bother you for a drink of water?"

"Sure," Mama told him, "just a minute and I'll get you one."

She walked over to the cupboard, reached for a glass, then filled the tumbler with water out of the fridge. But, instead of the stranger waiting at the door, when Mama turned around, he was standing right behind her, almost touching her. She gasped.

"Oh, I'm sorry I scared you," he said. "Do you live alone out here?"

"No," she said, "my husband's in bed, sleeping."

The hobo turned around, glanced in the bedroom, and saw Daddy asleep on the bed. The guy set the glass down on the counter, without even taking a drink, and rushed back out the door. I think that was the first time we were glad to see Daddy home, asleep on the bed during the day. The fact that he was there probably saved us from whatever the stranger had planned to do.

But, even at that, we knew Daddy would get up soon, and nobody knew what kind of a mood he'd be in. Maybe he'd take off for the bar, then we could relax for a while. I used to wonder why they ever stayed together. They never acted happy.

Later that day, when Daddy got up, I heard the words we all longed to hear.

"Hey, Reta, I'm gonna run up to the corner for a quick one."

Then he was gone. The other kids went out to play, but I stayed

DADDY NEVER CALLED ME PRINCESS

in the house and talked to Mama. Sometimes she'd talk about her old boyfriends. Her "old flames," she called them. I wondered why she never married any of them, if she loved them so much.

But I wanted to know about my real dad, I wanted to hear stories about him. Mama had promised to tell me that day and she was just getting started.

CHAPTER 18:
BILL

"When people walk away from you. Let them go, your destiny is never tied to anyone who leaves you, and it doesn't mean they are bad people. It just means that their part in your story is over."

- Beautifully Flawed

"You never forget your first love."

Mama told me about her first love. He sounded like a really great guy. They had lots of fun together. She even had his name tattooed on her leg so she would never forget him. They were planning to be married, but before that happened he got called into the service. She tearfully kissed him good-by and promised to wait. But I guess four years was too long to wait. She let her first love go, when she fell in love with someone else.

That someone else was Bill. They grew more in love as time passed and Bill asked her to move in with him. She said, "Yes." Even after they started living together, Bill never kept a steady job. Times were tough. But, no matter, they always had love, and because of that love, a little one was on the way.

The baby was a girl, and they named her Colleen. After Mama got her strength back, Bill took her on a bus trip to visit her parents. They had met Bill before. They also knew what Mama endured because of him, and they didn't approve. But they were overjoyed to meet their new grand-daughter. They took Mama aside and told

DADDY NEVER CALLED ME PRINCESS

her that she shouldn't traipse all over the country side with a new born, living from pillar to post. She promised Mama that if she'd leave the baby with her and Grandpa, just for awhile, that they would love and take real good care of her. She'd have plenty of food and anything else she needed. Then, when Bill got a steady job, and they had a home where they could settle down, she could come back for Colleen.

Mama knew Colleen would have a good home with her parents. She also knew that if she took her baby and went with Bill, she couldn't be sure if her baby would even get enough food, let alone anything else. Sometimes her and Bill only had apples to live on, for several days.

She talked it over with Bill, and explained that it would only be for a little while. Just until they could get back on their feet. Bill agreed to whatever Mama wanted. Because she loved her daughter, and only wanted the best for her, she sadly kissed her baby goodbye, and left with Bill.

They ended up living in the windy city of Chicago, in one small place after another. They'd find some little apartment, but when the rent was too far overdue, they'd have to leave. He was always looking for something to pawn off. One day Mama's beloved guitar came up missing. She didn't have to look far, it was as close as the nearest pawn shop. But she didn't have any money to buy her instrument back.

She stayed with Bill, I assumed, because she loved him. There never seemed to be a lack of money for drinking, but there was never enough for bills, or food. Bill and Mama were strolling around downtown. They walked by a place selling Chicago Coney Islands. Mama got whiff of a coney, which she loved with lots of onions and mustard. She started to drool.

"Oh, that smells delicious," she said.

"Let's go back," Bill answered.

Mama got all excited. She couldn't wait to sink her teeth into

BILL

one of the hot dogs. But Bill walked right on past the Coney Islands. "What are you doing?" Mama asked.

"Well, I just wanted to walk you by again, for another smell."

Sometimes the electric company shut off the power. Bill would scrounge around until he found something else to pawn, or sell for junk, so he could get it turned back on.

One night Mama was feeling extra depressed and contemplating whether she should leave Bill. Sometimes love just wasn't enough.

Bill was gone, so she went to bed alone. They didn't even have a fan, let alone air conditioning. She pushed her bed under an open window, hoping maybe she could draw in a little breeze, but there didn't seem to be any that night. She managed to fall asleep, despite the intense heat wave, when the ringing of the phone jarred her.

"Is this Reta?" The voice on the phone asked.

"Yes, this is her."

"Well, I'm calling from Cook County Hospital. Bill Becker was just brought in. We found your number in his wallet. He was in a hit and run an accident and he didn't survive. What do you want us to do with the body?"

Mama was in shock and heartbroken. She couldn't believe he was gone and she'd never see him again. She really did love him. She glanced at the clock, 2:30 P.M. She didn't have a car, or even any money for a taxi. She went in and threw herself across the bed as sobs racked her body. She didn't know what to do. Many confusing thoughts rushed through her mind. The night air had finally cooled and it felt great drifting in the open window. Mama had just fallen asleep when she was startled awake. A mans large hand stuck through the open window and grabbed her head. She screamed loud enough to wake the dead.

Then she heard laughter.

The laughter was coming from Bill, quite alive. He had just pulled another one of his many pranks on her.

DADDY NEVER CALLED ME PRINCESS

"I just wanted you to see how you'd feel if you really lost me," he said.

Mama was so angry, but her relief that he was alive overpowered the anger. When he came into the house she flew into his open arms. She forgave him, they kissed and made up.

Most of her stories made Bill seem like an awful man. Mama had such a hard life. I couldn't understand why she ever stayed with him. I started questioning why God would even let that happen. Why were we even born? Just to live for a few years, sometimes in a lot of pain, and then die and everything was over? What was the point of it all? What was the meaning of life? I worried, what if I ended up with a man who hurt me the way Mama had been hurt?

"You just take what you get, and deal with it," Mama said.

Time passed quickly. She could hardly believe it had been a year and a half since she'd left Colleen with her parents. Things were looking up, she went back to pick up her little girl.

"You can't take Colleen now," her mother said, "she's been with us so long. We love her."

"If you take her," her dad said, "you'll break your mother's heart. That would kill her."

Mama was devastated. She wanted her little girl back. But, on the other hand, she didn't want to break her mother's heart. They had raised her daughter and took good care of her far longer than planned. They both assured Mama that if she left Colleen with them they'd love her and she'd never want for anything. They could afford to give her all the things she'd ever need.

So, after a painful struggle, she asked them to drive her to the bus stop. She kissed her little girl good-bye, boarded the bus, and left her again.

Mama went back to Chicago. She found comfort in the arms of Bill, and shortly thereafter, she found herself pregnant again. She endured the changes in living quarters, the drinking and the many

BILL

pranks that Bill pulled, while trying to prepare for another child.

One hot, stuffy day in July, she went into labor. Because they didn't have a vehicle, and Bill was not around, she waddled around downtown looking for him. He was nowhere to be found. Mama had to ride to the hospital on a streetcar, and deliver her baby without him.

The proud Papa finally made an appearance, after he managed to find a larger place to bring his family back to, and the rent was paid up for thirty days. Things went well for awhile and she found pleasure in caring for their new little one.

A few months later their baby became sick. She was having trouble breathing, and nothing helped. Mama bundled the baby up, climbed on a street-car with Bill, and took her to the emergency room. The verdict was pneumonia and they had to leave her in the hospital. Mama was sad when she had to walk away from her little girl, in that tiny bed, under the oxygen tent.

Things were especially hard, because Christmas was only a few days away.

"Hey, Reta," Bill asked, "what do you want for Christmas?"

"All I want for Christmas," she said, "is my baby."

Bill went to hospital, on Christmas day, kidnapped the baby and took her home.

He walked in the door, with the baby in his arms, and handed her to Mama.

"Merry Christmas, honey," he said.

She was so happy to have her baby back home, all she could do was cry.

On one hand, that showed a tender, caring side of Bill. He wanted to give Mama the only thing she wanted for Christmas. But it also showed a complete lack of good judgment on his part. He could have put his daughter in grave danger. Mama endured a lot

DADDY NEVER CALLED ME PRINCESS

from Bill, and she did love him. But everyone has a breaking point and Mama finally reached hers. She took her baby and left to make a life of her own. That little girl would some day wonder if she'd ever get to meet Bill, her dad. I know, because that baby was me, and Bill was my dad.

CHAPTER 19:
THE SECOND TIME

"The sudden disappointment of a hope leaves a scar which the ultimate fulfillment of that hope never entirely removes."

- Thomas Hardy

Remember the day you turned thirteen?

Oh, how I longed to be a teenager. That meant I was growing up, no longer a little girl. I'd be starting high school soon, making new friends, getting to wear make-up. I'd heard that high school years were the best of your life. I couldn't wait to find our for myself.

I had been babysitting my sister and brothers for over a year. We no longer worried about other babysitters. Ma always went out and had a good time. She'd dress real pretty, getting ready for her night of dancing. She liked bright colors, lots of sparkles, and long, dangling earrings. For the final touch, she'd douse herself in Tabu perfume. Then she'd be off, trying her best to dance the night away. The next day, Ma would tell me about all the fun she'd had.

Other responsibilities were put on me. Ma would send me to the store with Daddy, so I could shop for the week's groceries. Daddy always gave me $20. Ma gave me a list: two cans of corn, two cans of peas, and two cans of green beans always topped the list, and seldom varied.

So with the list and money in hand, I'd head to the store with

DADDY NEVER CALLED ME PRINCESS

Daddy. Our first stop was always at the Cozy Corner Bar. I was old enough then, so I didn't have to wait in the car. Daddy would take me inside. I had to sit at a table and be quiet-he insisted. He'd sit at the counter, place his order, and include a pop for me. Sometimes, other people felt sorry for me and sent over drink refills and chips or something.

I tried to be seen and not heard. So I was sitting there, sipping my Coke, and minding my own business. When a fist was suddenly shaking in my face. It was attached to an angry drunk woman. She screamed at me.

"I saw you flirting with my husband, you little tramp! Well, if you want my husband, then you can just have him. He's all yours."

I had no idea who she was even talking about, let alone that I wanted him. I thought she was going to smack me. Daddy heard all the commotion and came over.

Hey, what's going on here?"

"She's been sitting there, flirting with my husband!"

"Oh, I don't think so, she doesn't even know how to flirt. She's only twelve years old."

Daddy got the lady calmed down. I was shaking in my shoes, and wondering why anyone enjoyed drinking. People acted much better when they were sober. Daddy finished his beer. We headed for the grocery store, I went in and Daddy waited in the car.

I tried to add up all the groceries in my head as I shopped, so I wouldn't go over the $20. When the cashier rang up $19.58, I breathed a sign of relief. I wouldn't have to be embarrassed by going through the items, trying to decide what to put back.

I was thankful we went straight home. I sure didn't want to run into the drunk lady who mistakenly thought I wanted her husband.

Back at home I changed into a pair of shorts. It was really hot, so I rolled up the cuffs. When I went in the living room Daddy looked at me and had a fit.

THE SECOND TIME

"You go change those shorts, right now! What are you trying to do? Entice boys?"

I was so hurt. Ma didn't see anything wrong with my shorts. I was only trying to cool off. I didn't even know what "entice" meant. But I went in and put on a dress.

Daddy left again, back to the Cozy Corner.

As I watched him pull out the drive I glanced at the neighbor's. I was hoping to get a glimpse of Joe, the boy next door. I'd had a crush on him ever since I could remember. He was a few years older than me, so we weren't in any of the same classes. If only he could just wait until I was a little older, instead of dating those other girls. I just watched him from afar, but something exciting was coming up. Joe was going to be on American Bandstand.

My eyes were glued to the television from the moment I heard Dick Clark's voice. Joe was somewhere in that crowd. The family was watching with me.

"There he is, there he is," we all yelled at the same time. Joe was dancing across the screen and he had a girl wrapped in his arms. That should have been me, wearing a Poodle skirt and Saddle Oxfords. I didn't take me eyes off the TV until American Bandstand was over.

My crush on Joe continued until my brother, Ronnie, washed his car one day.

"Hey, Wanda," he told me when he finished, "guess what I found in Joe's glove box?"

"Well, I have no idea," what did you find?"

"I found a package of something that boys carry in their wallets and use on girls."

"You big liar," I said, "you did not! Joe's not that kind of a guy."

But Ronnie convinced me that he was telling the truth. "Honest, Wanda," he said, "I really did." And that cured my crush

DADDY NEVER CALLED ME PRINCESS

on Joe.

Maybe I'd find someone else in school. I wanted to look like all the other girls with their modern hairdos. We didn't have money for haircuts, so my long hair just hung in a mess. Ma taught me how to curl it by rolling it up in rags, then tying it at the ends. That didn't help.

"Can you give me a haircut, Ma? So I'll look like the other girls?"

"Well I don't know how to cut hair," she said.

"Oh, sure you can, Ma. Just cut it short on the sides. Give me some long sweeping bangs. Layer it in the back. You can do it. I know you can. I'll get the scissors for you."

Ma kept insisting that she couldn't do it. I kept insisting that she could. She got tired of listening to me. I should have listened to her.

She wrapped a towel around my shoulders and started cutting. My long brown curls fell to the floor. I knew when I saw the finished cut it would be worth it. I'd finally fit in.

Snip, snip, then, "Ow," I said, when Ma slipped and cut my ear. But I sat there patiently.

"Okay," she said with a laugh. "I'm done."

When I looked in the mirror I was shocked. My hair was sticking up every which way, at least what little bit I had left. I started bawling.

"I told you I didn't know what I was doing." Ma said. "Maybe next time, you'll listen."

My only hope was that my older sister, Colleen, could help fix my hair. Daddy had to work on Saturday. We were going to Grandma and Grandpa's to celebrate my birthday. They were going to pick us up so we could spend the day.

We were ready when Grandpa came. Grandma stayed home to cook. She was a great cook. That's where Ma learned to cook so

THE SECOND TIME

well. She always made big meals, with plenty of foods. That day was no different. We walked in to a table set with lots of great smelling dishes: roasted chicken, mashed potatoes, corn, tossed salad, fruit salad, even Jello. And, of course, home baked rolls, with real butter. We only ate margarine at our house, so the butter tasted funny to me, but it made me feel rich. Everyone ate till they were stuffed. The grown-ups sat around talking, waiting for the food to settle, before we cut the cake. Grandma played the piano.

Colleen and I asked to be excused. We went in her bedroom so she could work on my hair. She didn't have a lot to work with, but she managed to make my new cut presentable.

"Thank you," I told her. "This is so exciting. I'm finally going to be a teenager."

"What do you mean? You're not going to be a teenager. You're only going to be twelve."

"Well, I don't think so. I've been twelve for the past year."

"No," she said, "you've only been eleven."

"I think I should know how old I am!"

"Well, if you don't believe me, go look it up in Grandma's Bible. Everyone's date of birth is listed in the front."

Colleen ran for Grandma's Bible. She laid it on the table, opened it up and pointed.

"See here, that's the date you were born. I told you. You're only going to be twelve."

I didn't believe her. Could that really be true? I ran in to show the Bible to Ma.

"According to this, I'm only going to be twelve years old, not thirteen. Is that right?"

Ma looked in the Bible. "Well, that's what it says, it must be right. We probably missed a year somewhere along the line."

"Well Ma! How could that even happen?"

DADDY NEVER CALLED ME PRINCESS

"Oh, I don't know," she said. "But you should be glad that you're not as old as you thought you were. And believe me, some day you'll thank me."

My heart sunk down to my toes. How could a mother forget the year her child was born? I felt like she didn't care at all. I knew that I had gained a year, but at the time, I felt like a year of my life had just been ripped away. I'd have to wait another twelve months before I'd be a teenager. Suddenly, I was a little girl again. Maybe I'd be able to thank her, someday, but certainly not on the day I turned twelve, for the second time.

CHAPTER 20:
FURY BREEDS FURY

"Children have never been very good at listening to their elders, but they have never failed to imitate them."

- James A. Baldwin

We all felt bad for Ronnie. He received the worst of Daddy's fury, next to Ma. Maybe Ronnie reminded Daddy too much of himself, even at age ten. They were both as bullheaded as the bull that cornered Penny and me on our way to the store. But even though Daddy gave Ronnie plenty of reasons to cry, he refused to shed a tear, it only fueled his anger against his dad.

Once, when Daddy was mad at him, he beat Ronnie over the head with a piece of aluminum antenna pipe. He noticed that he had bent the pipe, so he turned it over and beat Ronnie on the head again to straighten it out.

My brother, Rodney, was so gentle and easy going that he never got hit. Us girls, well, we tried our best not to make Daddy mad. But Ronnie didn't seem to care.

Penny was very tenderhearted and easily hurt. Daddy could make her cry with just one look. Ronnie had been sneaking in Ma's homemade jar of jelly. Daddy saw the fingerprints and went looking for the culprit. Penny took the blame, just to keep Ronnie from getting whipped.

"Oh, thank you," Ronnie told her. "You're the best sister ever."

DADDY NEVER CALLED ME PRINCESS

Daddy didn't hit us girls with his hands, he used angry words and other kinds of abuse.

"Get down on the floor, Penny," he'd say. Penny would look so sad. But she'd do what Daddy told her to. She'd crouch down on her little hands and knees.

"Now bark like a dog," he'd order.

She'd try to make little barking sounds, but pretty soon she'd break down and cry. That only made Daddy laugh. "Oh look," he'd say, "she's going to cloud up and rain all over."

Ronnie liked to dream up wild stunts. And, more often than not, he'd use our little brother, Rodney, for his test runs. He'd rig up some weird contraption so he could play detective. After he'd gather up all the belts he could find, he'd strap Rodney in what he called his "electric chair." He'd tie lots of wires across the top of Rodney's head and around his fingers. He'd hook the wires up to light bulbs and batteries, then he'd give Rodney a lie detector test. Whenever he asked a question, if he didn't get the right answer, he'd say, "No, that's a lie!" Then he'd rub the wires together giving Rodney a shock. But Rodney loved his big brother so much he'd let him do anything. And no one wanted to tell Daddy. We didn't like to see Ronnie get into trouble.

Ronnie started a club house. Before anyone could join, they had to pass his initiation. The first test would be to walk his tightrope, some rope tied between a couple of trees. If the walker didn't pass his test, he'd hit them in the legs with a picker bush. The club was never very large.

Ronnie spent a lot of time searching the neighborhood, looking for junk to use for his many inventions. One of his friend's dad had some old army equipment stored in his basement. Ronnie got a hold of one of the gas masks. He dug a big hole out back behind some trees. He went into the house and got the ladder from his bunk bed then stuck it down the hole. He threw a bunch of sticks and twigs in a pile on the dirt floor. Then he crawled down the hole and set everything on fire. He let it burn for a little bit, then he doused the fire with a pail of water until black smoke rolled upward. He convinced his friends, one at a time, to put on the gas mask and crawl down into the hole. He timed them to see who could stay down there the longest. When the smoke died down, he started all over with the fire and the water til smoke rolled again.

Ronnie got into a lot of fights at school, people called him a trouble maker. I think he wanted to take his anger out on Daddy for hurting Ma. Ronnie would stand in the background, stiff legged, with his hands clenched. He'd watch with a look of pure hatred in his eyes for our dad. Ronnie wasn't big enough then to stop him, but we knew that some day he would be.

Daddy came home one day with a surprise for all of us. He had bought a small cabin up by Lake George and he wanted to take us all up there for a week. Since we rarely went anywhere it promised to be a real treat. We were so excited. Ma packed all the stuff we'd need, and us kids loaded up the car. The best part was that since Daddy had to work, he was going to drop us all off while he went back and worked all week, then he'd come back for us on the weekend. Daddy said the cabin was close enough to the lake that we could walk. We didn't have swimming suits but we could swim in our shorts. It wasn't like we were going to a pool where we'd be embarrassed because we didn't dress like all the other kids.

So on Saturday morning we climbed in the car and off we went. After what seemed like forever, Daddy pulled in front of the cabin. It was brand new, but small and not finished yet. There was only one big room and a small bathroom, but we could have fun. We wanted to see the lake and they said we could go. We were the only ones down there. We didn't find the pretty beach we were looking for. Instead, we saw a lot of water with a little sand hauled in. Eventually it would be made into a beach. The water looked deep and we couldn't go out too far or it would have been over our heads. I had to watch Rodney real close, he was only 4 at the time. But at least we could cool off and splash around.

Daddy stayed that first night. It was weird with all of us sleeping in the same room. Ma & Daddy had a bed, but us kids

DADDY NEVER CALLED ME PRINCESS

slept on the floor.

The next morning Daddy took Ma to buy enough groceries to last us the week, then he left and headed back home. He'd come back for us on Saturday.

We had fun all week, checking out the place, going for walks. Most of the cabins were new, I loved the smell of the wood, and not many people lived there yet. It seemed like everyone came up to work on their place on the week-ends. Through the week the area seemed deserted. We enjoyed getting in the water but since it was so deep, we couldn't go out very far. There was a little store that was close enough to walk to. We had enough change for some Penny candy.

Saturday came far too soon, but Daddy didn't. Ma said he was probably waiting until Sunday. Then Sunday came, but again, Daddy never showed up. Ma was getting worried.

"I wonder when he plans on coming," she said, "we're almost out of food."

We thought he'd surely be there on Monday, but he wasn't. Ma had just enough change to walk down to the pay phone and call him. We all went with her and stood around, waiting to hear what Daddy said. He didn't say anything, he never answered.

"Well," Ma said, "I don't know what's keeping him, but I hope he comes pretty soon. Maybe I can scrounge around and find something for us to eat today. Then I don't know what we're going to do."

The next day Ronnie and Penny took off by themselves to play. I stayed home and talked to Ma and we both tried to keep Rodney entertained.

"Ronnie and Penny have been gone quite a while," Ma said. "They better get back here pretty soon or I'll have to go look for them." As soon as she spoke the words, the door opened and they both walked in. They were each carrying a bag of groceries.

FURY BREEDS FURY

"Where in the world did you get the groceries?" Ma asked.

"We couldn't let everyone go hungry," Ronnie said. "So we went around to all the empty cabins. We found bottles laying around in the yard. Some places we could see bottles on the porch, so we broke in the screen doors and took them. We found so many bottles. We couldn't carry them all at once so we made a few trips. We got 2 cents each and ended up with $20."

"You know it's not right to steal, but maybe God will forgive you, He knows we sure needed the food. Let's see what you got. There was a big box of spaghetti, some spaghetti sauce, a loaf of bread, some lunch meat, a small bottle of mustard, some toilet paper, and a bottle of Dish Soap, because they knew Ma liked to be clean.

My stretched the food until Daddy finally picked us up, a whole week late. I don't even remember the reason he gave. But he must have felt guilty, because he gave us kids some money and said we could go to the movies by ourselves when we got home. We could hardly wait. Everyone said the theater was so much fun, and we'd have a chance to find out for ourselves.

Back at home, we unpacked, took off behind the house and headed for the woods. We ran all the way to the other side of the golf course, hoping we'd get there in time for the next show. We didn't have to watch the others with a hopeful longing, like we used to do. We stood in line and had money for tickets. The popcorn, with all the butter, smelled so good when we walked in the door. The man took our tickets and pointed the way to the giant screen. I was amazed. The film playing that day was "The Sad Horse," a family drama movie about a depressed race horse and a lonely boy becoming best friends. We sat there in awe, spellbound, with all the sights and sounds of the big screen, enjoying our very first movie.

When it was over, most of us walked out with tears running down our faces. Except for one little red-haired, freckle-faced boy, Ronnie. His eyes were dry. We headed home and I couldn't help but wonder what was going on inside his little brain. Didn't he think the

DADDY NEVER CALLED ME PRINCESS

movie was sad? Or maybe it was because he had seen so much worse. Then I remembered him watching Ma get beat and how he reacted. Maybe he had closed off all his emotions and put up walls. The strangeness of the electric chair and the gas masks that he used for play, Daddy seemed to be the trigger for it all. Maybe Ronnie was deep in thought, seriously plotting how to get his next revenge on Daddy.

CHAPTER 21:
BREWING FOR A FIGHT:

"Long term domestic violence: Being abused in this manner is like being kidnapped and tortured for ransom but you will never have enough to pay off the kidnapper."

- Rebecca J. Burns...The Last Straw

    The day was Saturday. Daddy didn't have to work, so he'd been home all day. The only noise that could be heard was Daddy, upstairs on his Ham Radio. He was so involved, talking with someone from out of state, and he didn't want to shut it down. He'd hollered for so many beers and we knew the empties would be piling up. We figured a fight was soon to follow. As a thirteen year old I didn't know what to do to stop it from happening. I felt helpless. The other kids couldn't be much help either. Ronnie was ten, Penny eight, and Rodney only four.

    We had to sit still and be quiet. We couldn't even laugh, for fear that we'd disturb his conversation and he'd yell at us, or make us go sit on our bed for hours. We barely even dared to move. While trying to read one of my Modern Romance magazines it was hard to focus and I dreaded what was sure to come. The other kids were quietly drawing pictures. Mama was always dusting or baking. When Daddy gave his call letters, signaling that he was coming downstairs, Mama sent us kids outside to play.

    Daddy signed off and shut down his Ham Radio. Big heavy boots stomped down the stairs as we filed out the door, followed by

DADDY NEVER CALLED ME PRINCESS

his deep, scary voice. We could hear him clear outside. "Hey, why did everybody run off?"

Ronnie and I got a couple of empty beer cases out of the shed and drug them to the house. Standing on top of the cartons brought us in line with the kitchen window. We could peek through the crack in the curtains and make out the forms of Mama & Daddy. Penny insisted on watching and she could see if she stood on her tip toes. Rodney was too young and I didn't think he needed to watch anyway. We hid behind the house and listened, almost afraid to breathe. Rodney kept tugging on my skirt.

"Hey, Wanda, what's going on?"

We huddled together outside the window and caught glimpses of them. Sure enough, the fighting started. The screaming and cussing was even worse than usual. He slapped Ma across the face once, then again & again. She kept swearing at him too, and she refused to shut up. He put both of his hands around her throat, pushed her back against the stove and started choking her. We all watched in helpless horror as Mama started to turn blue. She couldn't breathe. Penny and I cried in a panic, fearing for our mother's life. Ronnie doubled up his fist and leaned in for a closer glare of hatred. If looks could kill, then Daddy would have been facing eternity.

"Just wait till I'm bigger," he said, "Daddy won't beat on her then."

Should we run down the country road? I wondered. Could we find someone with a phone and call the police?

But we stood by and watched helplessly as Daddy beat Mama and there was not a thing any of us could do.

Mama was not so helpless. Although Daddy was much bigger & stronger, Mama did her best to fight back. She reached behind her and grabbed one of the heavy steel grates off the gas stove. She raised the black stove piece high in the air, brought it down with a slam and hit Daddy over the head. He let go of her throat and

BREWING FOR A FIGHT:

staggered backwards. He looked like he was going to pass out. Blood was running down his face, he wiped it off with the back of his hand. He shook his head then came at her again.

"Go ahead!" she screamed, "if that makes you feel like a man, but so help me, I'll bash your head in!"

They wrestled and swore at each other several more times... Then... finally...it was over.

"That's enough, you crazy red head," Daddy said, "now get over there and cook me a steak."

Mama threw his steak in a pan then came outside to check on us. Her face was all swollen and bruised, but she wasn't even crying. She rarely ever cried, at least not on the outside. She was a strong, tough woman and very stubborn. I guess she'd learned that through the years as a way to survive.

"Are you alright, Mama?" I asked.

"I'll be okay," she said.

"Why don't you just leave him?"

"I don't have any money and we don't have anyplace else to go."

"Well when I get married," I promised her, "you can all come and live with me."

"That would be nice, Sweetie, someday. But he's cooled down for now. After he eats his steak he'll just pass out. Then you kids can come back in the house."

Soon to follow would be the part where Daddy would do something nice for Mama, trying to make up. He seemed to know that the way to her heart was through her kids, so sometimes he'd surprise us and pull Milky Way's out of his pocket. But that night, as much as I loved candy, I didn't want a Milky Way, or anything else, from him.

Mama went back in the house. We just sat quietly on the beer cartons until Daddy passed out. Mama came and got us, then we

DADDY NEVER CALLED ME PRINCESS

went into the house and got ready for bed. I tried so hard to go to sleep, but my mind wouldn't turn off. I couldn't relax. I knew that Penny, lying right beside me, was awake too. All I could think about was Mama and all the ways that Daddy hurt her. I couldn't help but wonder how long it would be until the next fight. I could only hope that the beatings would stop.

CHAPTER 22:
KIDS NEED ATTENTION

"The truth is, attention seekers are looking for validation. They want to know that they are worthy."

- Unknown

"Hey, everyone, come on outside," Ronnie hollered, "I want to show you something."

We all ran out to see what he wanted, except Rodney, we didn't know where he was.

"Look up here," Ronnie yelled.

Daddy had a really high tower that he used for his Ham Radio equipment. We all looked up to see that Ronnie had climbed to the top of Daddy's tower. It was just after dark, and we couldn't see real well, but we could make out a vague outline of him. He had a lit cigarette dangling from his mouth. And he had Rodney up there with him.

"Look! He made Rodney climb up there too." I said.

"Ronnie! Ma hollered "you're going to give me a heart attack. You get down here, right this minute!"

"Okay," he said, then he picked Rodney up in the air and threw him off the tower. Rodney landed on the ground with a thump. We screamed and Ma almost passed out.

Just then, Rodney came around the corner laughing. Ronnie had

DADDY NEVER CALLED ME PRINCESS

only pretended to throw him off. In reality, he'd only thrown off a stuffed dummy.

Ronnie would do anything to get a little attention, good, or bad. Like the day that Ma was outside working on her flowers. I had just picked a pail of berries and was on my way into the house when I heard screams. The voices seemed to be coming from upstairs, but we never used the upstairs. Daddy had a 4×8 sheet of plywood covering the access hole. I ran around the house to see what all the noise was about. What I saw put pure panic in my heart and sent the pail of berries flying. Rodney was dangling against the house, outside the open window. Ronnie was holding him by his arms.

"What do you think you're doing?" I yelled.

"Help!" He said. "He's slipping!"

"Hold on," I screamed.

"Ma! Ma! Come quick!" She came around the corner.

"What's all the racket about?" she asked.

"Look," I said, as I pointed to the upstairs window, where Rodney was dangling down the side of the house.

Ma looked up, "Rodney, how in the world did you climb up the side of that house?"

Ma shot into the house with us right behind her. Ronnie had slid the sheet of plywood back to expose the hole. Ma climbed the stairs in a flash and pulled Rodney back inside. We all breathed a huge sigh of relief, especially, Rodney.

"What were you trying to do?" she asked Ronnie.

"Well," he said, "I told Rodney to climb out the window for a joke and then I'd pull him back in. But he was too heavy and I couldn't get him back in."

"You could have killed your brother," she said, then grounded him for a week.

Ma had her hands full, dealing with all of Ronnie's stunts, as if

KIDS NEED ATTENTION

putting up with Daddy's' beatings wasn't enough. Penny and I certainly caused Ma our share of trouble, too, on top of everything else. The combination of things was taking a toll on her, and adding to her gray hairs.

One night, after the other kids were in bed, Ma wanted to have a serious talk with me.

"Wanda," she said, "sometimes I feel like I'm going crazy. So I want you to watch me. Hard to tell what I'd do if I had a nervous breakdown. I might try to pick one of the kids up and throw them in the fireplace or something. Just keep an eye on me. Do whatever you have to do. Grab something and hit me over the head with it. The fireplace poker, or whatever it takes. Just stop me! Please, don't let me do anything to hurt any of them."

So I told Ma not to worry, that I'd keep an eye on her. And for a long time after that, I never pulled my eyes away. I watched with fear in my heart, praying that she'd never do anything. I could not even entertain the fact of possibly having to knock out my mother.

I hardly slept at all that night. The next day, Ma said she needed to get away for awhile. after all that us kids put her through. She wanted to go visit her friend down the road.

"And you kids are going with me." She said. "I have to keep a close eye on all of you. But I deserve a little fun too. I think I'll take a case of your dad's beer along. Ronnie, you grab one end, Wanda, you grab the other end."

She held Rodney's hand and Penny followed beside. We walked the mile to her friend's house, who was glad to see us coming, especially with that case of Drewrey's we were carrying.

Ma and her friend talked and laughed and the time got away from them. Her friend's husband would be coming home and her cleaning wasn't finished. She had a house full of rugs and wanted to know if I'd shake them for her. She'd pay me 25 cents each.

I hated shaking rugs, with sand and dirt flying in my face. But I sure liked the money, so I said yes. After that, she'd call me over,

DADDY NEVER CALLED ME PRINCESS

every now and again, and hire me to shake rugs.

I didn't like getting dirty, I wanted to look nice, but Ma said I spent too much time primping in the mirror. She came up with a poem that her mom used to repeat to her.

"Bathroom hog, you primp and fuss, but always look the same to us.

It isn't worth the time you take, your face is just a big mistake."

Her poem never stopped me from trying to look my best. With every new hair style I'd ask, "Hey, Ma, do you like my hair this way?" And I'd try my best to grab her attention again.

CHAPTER 23:
HEY, STINKY

"Sticks and stones may break a bone, but words can break a heart."
                                                  - Stephen D. Glass

Everyone called him "Stinky."

Ronnie hated the nickname, but, at least for one day, the name certainly fit. One of Ronnie's jobs was to dump, "the pot." He had to carry it out and dump it in the outhouse. We were sitting in the living room, playing hide the button. Ronnie walked through to get the throne. He had to walk by us to get outside. We all held our nose. The smell was putrid.

"Hurry up, Ronnie," Ma said, "and get that stinking thing out of here."

Ronnie carried it outside. We heard screams, so we all ran out to look. Ronnie had tripped, going down the steps, and fell. He had dumped "the pot," right on top of his head. Brown toilet paper was hanging from his ears.

"It burns! It burns!" He yelled.

"Well you're not coming back in this house smelling like that," Ma said. "Get over there by the hose so you can clean yourself off."

Ma put some water on to heat, after the worst was cleaned off, so Ronnie could have a sponge bath and be allowed back in the house.

DADDY NEVER CALLED ME PRINCESS

Kids are cruel, and we were no different with the name calling. I guess when you're young you don't realize how much that hurts.

Ma never had money to take us for haircuts, she even cut her own hair. I can still see her in my mind and hear her saying. "Time for a haircut." She'd sit down in her chair with the scissors. She never even looked in a mirror. She'd just pull her hair out away from her head and start cutting. She'd have a trash bag beside her to throw the hair in. When she felt like she'd cut enough, she'd say,

"Okay, I'm done."

And amazingly, her self done haircuts worked, she always looked good.

I acquired the job of cutting the rest of the families hair. All except for Daddy, he seemed to find money for the barbershop.

I didn't do too bad of a job on Penny's hair. At least she always said she liked the cut. But when I'd cut Ronnie and Rodney's hair, well, that was a different story. We didn't have hair clippers, so I'd use scissors and a comb. After wrapping an old towel around their head, I'd start cutting, first one side, then the other. And I'd go over their head again, trying my best to even things up. But, try as I might, whenever I was finished, they always looked like they'd been scalped. They'd run and hide behind the couch. We'd chant, in unison, while we laughed at them.

"Butch and Baldy. Butch and Baldy."

"You're never cutting my hair again." They'd each yell

But of course, six weeks later, I'd grab the scissors and take another whack at them. But I never quite got the hang of being a beautician, even though I had to cut my own long brown hair.

Being the only one with brown hair, in a family of redheads, was hard. People would ask,"Well, where did you come from, the milkman?"

I was so tall and skinny, people called me, "Bean Pole." If I stood sideways, Ma would say, "Move your arm, I can't see your

HEY, STINKY

waist."

We all had freckles. So "Freckle Face," was a popular name. And once, someone even asked if we were standing behind a screen when someone threw cow dung.

I remember scrubbing my face so hard, with lemons. But that never worked.

When Ma was young, people called her, "Carrot Top." She also grew up in a poor family, and the kids called her "Poor Little Reta." Ma told me about a time she went to the ice cream shop with some friends. She stood behind them and watched as they each ordered an ice cream cone, chocolate, strawberry, or vanilla.

"Poor Little Reta can't afford any ice cream." She heard one of them whisper.

The lady behind the counter finished serving cones to Ma's friends. Then she looked at Ma and asked, "And what kind of an ice cream do you want?"

"I don't want any." Ma said.

"Well sure you do." The lady answered.

"No," Ma whispered, "I don't have any money."

The lady smiled, leaned over the counter, and whispered back.

"That's okay," she said, "just pick out any flavor you like, it's on me."

Ma was almost drooling. But she didn't have a favorite, she liked them all.

The lady made up a cone with not one, or even two, but with three huge dips of ice cream, one of each flavor. And much to the surprise of all her friends, she handed the cone to Ma. The cone was bigger than any of them were licking.

"Well, look what Reta's got," she heard them say, "and she didn't even have to pay."

DADDY NEVER CALLED ME PRINCESS

Ma never forgot the kind lady who worked at the ice cream parlor. People seem to remember anything that makes an impact on them, good, or bad.

Ma said we'd just have to learn to live with all the different names that people called us. "Just remember how that feels," she'd say, "and don't do the same to others. You can't do anything about the looks you were born with, so learn to make the best of what you do have."

But there was one name that Ma said we could do something about.

"We might not have much money," she said, "but we have soap and water. You can always take care of your bodies, and keep them clean. Then, at least you won't have to worry about anyone calling you, "Stinky."

CHAPTER 24:
TICKET TO ESCAPE

"Auto racing is boring except when a car is going at least 172 miles per hour upside down."

- Dave Berry

Daddy would travel several hundred miles to watch races. In fact, every year, Daddy took Ma to see the Indianapolis 500-Mile Race. Once, they even saw a driver get killed during one of the races. Sometimes riding mechanics or track people, could be killed in practice. A few spectators even lost their lives. Racing sounded dangerous to me.

But it never killed Daddy's love for the sport. He shared a love for the races with some of his drinking buddies. "Hey, Lyle," one of his friends had asked, "I'm taking the wife and kids to the races tonight. How about you bring your family and come along with us?"

So that's how Daddy, Ma, my two brothers, sister and I, ended up sitting in the top of the bleachers, waiting for the races to begin. We were so high up, it made me dizzy just to look over the edge. And if anyone dropped something through the cracks, it was gone. The price of admission was cheaper for kids under thirteen, so even after my thirteenth birthday, when Daddy took us to the races, I was still twelve. That night, although I couldn't admit it, I was fifteen.

I didn't like watching the cars crash, like my brothers did, but I enjoyed hot dogs with all the fixings, washed down with ice-cold

DADDY NEVER CALLED ME PRINCESS

Coke. I also liked to watch the people with their cameras and gigantic lenses. At the end of the race they took pictures of the happy winners signing autographs. Watching people get so excited over winning was the best part. Penny thought being around a crowd of people was the most fun. Daddy and his friend busied themselves by passing around and guzzling cold beers. For different reasons, we all enjoyed our nights at Auto City, or sometimes at Dixie Motor Speedway.

They handed each of us a ticket when we came in the gate, with a chance at winning the prize. I gripped a ticket in my sweaty palm, hoping against hope, that I held a winner. Then I could run through the crowd, as I'd watched many do before, and accept the prize.

Daddy didn't care about the drawing. He just liked the cars, motorcycles, noise, racing, demolishing; it didn't matter. He loved everything about speed. Ma said it was just his way to escape life, along with the drinking. Sometimes, I wish I had a way to escape.

People all around were boozing it up, some of them loudly cussing. Time trials were over. Everyone stood when they played the National Anthem. The flag went down and cars took off. The noise was deafening. Fans yelled and screamed.

"Punch it! To the floor!" Daddy yelled, "The inside track."

"Slam him out-of-place," his friend said. "Plenty of guts."

"Lots of hotheads out there," came from somewhere in the crowd.

Ma stood up once and spilled beer all over the guy in front of her. He jumped up, shocked at first, then he laughed and brushed beer off his clothes. I just endured it all, and clung to the ticket in my hand, waiting...

Finally, it was time for the drawing.

Cars had stopped, we were right in the middle of half-time. They were about to draw the winning ticket. Everyone got silent as numbers blared from the loud-speaker, 2 3 4 1 6 7.

TICKET TO ESCAPE

Penny screamed!

My sister won, even thought I didn't, I was happy for her. She was so excited. That was the first time she'd ever won anything. She hurried down to claim the prize. Her red pony tails flopped from side to side as she bounced down the bleachers. Her freckled face showed signs from being too long in the sun. She accepted her gift amidst cheers from the crowd. She climbed back up that enormous set of stairs holding a little Brownie Kodak Camera.

I was more excited that she was. I longed for a camera. Anyone listening to us would have thought we were on a debate team. I reminded her that I was five years older, and the only one who could afford to buy film. She knew how bad I wanted to take pictures.

And then Penny, with her soft heart, turned the camera over to me. I tore open the box, loaded the camera, and stood in front of them to take my very first picture. I tried to center Penny, Rodney, and Ronnie in the middle, with the race track showing in the background. They looked at me and smiled, then click.

A new love was born for me.

My personal way to escape. I had thoughts of being able to capture tons of memories. I had visions of getting older and graduating to bigger and better cameras. I would take so many pictures that when we all grew up and had homes of our own, I'd go to visit and see my pictures on their walls. Whenever I'd hear the words, "wedding," "new house," "baby," or even someone's "black eye," I could be right there with my camera in hand. My heart filled with joy just thinking about all the possibilities. And maybe, someday, I'd even have grand kids to take pictures of. They'd probably get tired of hearing me say the word, "smile," so often. But what would life be without pictures to capture all the best times?

My sister, Penny, started it all. I imagined searching garage sales, flea markets, even auctions, trying to find another little camera like the one she gave me. When I found it, I planned to wrap that little

DADDY NEVER CALLED ME PRINCESS

Brownie Kodak with a big red bow, and give it back to Penny.

"Thanks, sis," I'd say, "for giving me a way to escape. I love ya."

On that one special night at the races I had a lot of big dreams. I felt like such a grown-up. Maybe, I remember thinking, I would even be able to start dating soon, because after all, I had my very own camera and I wasn't a kid anymore.

CHAPTER 25:

LUCKY

"The magic of first love is our ignorance that it can never end."

- Benjamin Disraeli

"I Wanna Be Bobby's Girl."

"You're not a kid anymore," as the song goes. I was almost sixteen and I didn't want to turn sweet sixteen and never been kissed. All the other girls had boyfriends. I wouldn't feel complete until I belonged to some guy, although Daddy didn't think I was old enough.

Ma remembered what it was like to be young and she was all for me getting a boyfriend. But with Daddy that was out of the question. So I came up with a plan.

Pipeline. Everyone else was doing it. You got on the phone and dialed a certain number. The number always rang busy, but you just stayed on the line. If you listened real well, between the beeps of the busy signal, you could hear people talking. When some guy thought you sounded good he'd ask for your number. If you liked the sound of him then you gave him your number. You just hollered out real loud, between the beeps. Then he called and you could have a normal conversation.

Many hours were spent on the Pipeline when Daddy was gone. Some guy finally asked,

"What's...your...number?"

DADDY NEVER CALLED ME PRINCESS

I yelled out my number. We hung up and he called right away. My first phone call ever, from a guy. His name was Lucky. He sounded pretty nice and he only lived about 8 miles away. He was a year older than me and went to a school across town. We talked for several hours, then every night that followed, for many more hours. We decided to meet. I warned him ahead of time that if he ever saw Daddy's car in the drive not to come around. Since he didn't have a car he was going to walk over to my house. He was on his way.

Ma, Ronnie, Penny, Rodney and I were watching out the window for him. I was so nervous. I didn't even know what he looked like. We finally spotted some guy walking down the road who didn't look familiar. I couldn't bear to watch, so I went in my bedroom. Everyone else watched for me.

"Oh, Wanda," Ma yelled. "Here comes the homeliest guy I've ever seen."

The neighborhood dogs started barking. Someone knocked on the door and Ma invited him in. I could hear them talking and I thought he sounded pretty good.

"Someone's here to meet you," Ma yelled.

I gathered my courage, looks aren't everything, and walked to the door. When I saw him standing there my heart did flip flops. I was face to face with the most gorgeous guy. He was taller than me and had a slim build. Blond wavy hair tumbled into sea-blue eyes. He had long eyelashes that would make any girl jealous. He was wearing jeans and a black leather jacket.

He held out his hand, "Hi, Wanda, I'm Lucky."

His smile was more than I could have hoped for. I assumed, by the look in his eyes, that he was pleased with what he saw in me. I got a whiff of his after shave and I loved the smell.

I introduced him to all my family. Ma invited him to eat with us then put supper on the table. He raved about Ma's cooking, and rightfully so, she had even scrimped on other things so she could have pork chops that night. After supper we all sat in the living

LUCKY

room. Lucky made a big hit with my brothers when he showed them some magic tricks. He won me over as he kept glancing my way and flashing his gorgeous smile. By the time he left that evening, my whole world had changed. I think even the angels smiled.

After that, Lucky walked over to see me, or hitched a ride, every chance he got. We were never able to go out anywhere, but my family and I got to know him pretty well. I was falling faster with every meeting. He asked for my picture to carry in his wallet. He didn't think I combed my hair with an egg beater, like Daddy said. He told me I was pretty and the nicest girl he'd ever known.

We were walking around outside one evening. We stopped and sat down at the picnic table. Ma sent Ronnie out with some iced tea for us. We took the tea, then Lucky told Ronnie he'd give him a quarter if he'd leave. Ronnie took the quarter and happily ran off.

"You always look so pretty, Wanda," Lucky said. "Other girls fix up only when they go out, but you fix up nice and wear a dress every day. You look just like a princess."

He called me Princess? And for the very first time, I felt like a princess.

He wrapped his arm around me for a hug, then patted my back. He took my chin in his hand and tilted my face towards him. I could have gotten lost in those sea-blue eyes. I knew it was coming. All I'd been dreaming about was my first kiss, and then he kissed me. It wasn't a deeply passionate kiss, like you see in the movies, but oh, so sweet. I even kissed him back.

"Wanda," he said, "I'm falling for you, more every day, would you be my steady girl?"

I eagerly said, "yes." and he placed his ring on my finger. I wouldn't be able to wear the ring around Daddy, but that was okay, I had a boyfriend.

I turned sixteen a few days later and it wasn't sweet sixteen and never been kissed. Lucky sang "Happy Birthday Sweet Sixteen," by

DADDY NEVER CALLED ME PRINCESS

Neil Sedaka. Daddy didn't know I already had a boyfriend but Ma convinced him I was old enough. He agreed that I could see a guy, just as long as we only saw each other at home.

The next time Lucky walked over he was carrying a bunch of wild flowers. I didn't even mind when he walked in and handed them to Ma, and no, she didn't throw them in the garbage, like she did Daddy's. She put the flowers in a tall jelly jar and set them in the middle of the table.

Daddy was home and I introduced him to Lucky. Daddy didn't like him from the beginning. I could tell by the way he eyed him up and down. Lucky didn't stay long after that. Later I could hear Daddy talking to Ma.

"I don't know what she sees in that kid," he said, "with that black leather jacket he looks like a hoodlum. He probably belongs to some gang."

"Now, Lyle," Ma said, "at least give the guy a chance."

Lucky still came around, far more often than we told about. He wanted to know what Daddy thought of him. Ronnie piped up, "He thinks you belong to some motorcycle gang with that black jacket of yours."

Lucky wanted to please Daddy so he dug a hole and buried his jacket, at least that's what he said. Daddy didn't believe that he really buried it and he hated liars. Daddy still wasn't happy.

Lucky made me happy. I'd watch out the window and wait for him to walk up the road. Not even bad weather stopped him. "Rain or shine, gotta see that girl of mine," he'd say. With all the compliments and attention I felt very special. We went together for over a year. We didn't believe others when they said it was only puppy love. Puppy love is real, at least for the puppy. He asked me to marry him. If we'd been older I'd have ran off with him, but I knew Daddy wouldn't stand for that. I also didn't want to leave and make it harder on Ma and the other kids.

Lucky was over at the house one day when Daddy was home.

LUCKY

They were talking to each other and Daddy asked him something about an electric bill. Lucky told him about a huge bill that his parents had received.

"I don't think they ever got a bill that large," Daddy said.

Lucky held to his story, trying to convince Daddy that he was telling the truth.

Daddy wasn't convinced, he was furious. He jumped out of his chair, ran over and grabbed Lucky by the throat. "Don't lie to me. You little SOB!"

No one ever dared lie to Daddy, or they paid, big time. His face was all red and he kept shaking Lucky and slamming him into the wall. Ma tried to pull him away.

"Stop," she said, "you're going to kill him."

"You get out of here, now," he gave Lucky one hard shove, "and don't ever come back."

Daddy looked at me. "You choose!" he said, "Him, or me? If you choose him, you can leave right now. You'll never be welcome in this house again."

Since we were both underage, with no jobs, or even a car, what else could I do? I pictured Lucky and me, walking out into the night, broke and alone.

I told Daddy I'd stay. Lucky walked out of my life. I didn't know if I'd ever see him again.

I wasn't really surprised that Daddy got so mad when he thought Lucky lied to him, but there was probably more to it than that. I think he'd just been looking for a way to break us up.

That evening I got a phone call from Lucky. He was crying.

"Wanda?" he sniffed, "Wanda?"

I didn't dare answer. With a broken heart, I silently hung up. He didn't call back.

DADDY NEVER CALLED ME PRINCESS

Daddy would come home at strange hours, trying to catch me, so it was impossible to sneak around and meet my best friend, Lucky. I never knew love could hurt so much. I cried many tears as I listened to Neil Sedaka singing—"Breakin' Up Is Hard To Do." People told me,

"Oh, he was only your first love, you'll get over him. You'll find someone else."

I didn't believe them, I didn't want anyone else. I wanted my first love. I wondered if I'd ever see him again, because I knew I'd never get over Lucky.

CHAPTER 26:
FIVE FINGER DISCOUNT

"The only thing worth stealing is a kiss from a sleeping child."

- Joe Houldsworth

"Penny's at the police station?"

Ma and I had been sitting on the couch talking when she got a phone call. Her face turned white before she hung up. "Yes," she said, "and now I have to go upstairs and tell your dad that they caught his eleven year old daughter shop lifting. He'll have to pick her up and he's going to kill her." She told Daddy and he took off like a Bloodhound on a scent.

"I can't believe Penny would steal," I said.

"Me neither, but she was caught red-handed, along with that friend of hers, Shelly. I knew that girl was bad news when she started hanging around here."

"I wonder what she stole?"

"I don't know," Ma said, "but whatever it was, she's not going to think it was worth it when her Dad gets a hold of her. Now I'm wondering about all that stuff she gave everyone last week. I loved my new dish rags, and the boys loved their toys and trucks."

"Yeah, and she gave me mascara, 'so you'll look pretty,' she said, 'for the new boyfriend you'll get.' But she said she found $20 in the parking lot."

DADDY NEVER CALLED ME PRINCESS

"I know that's what she said, but I thought that was kind of funny when she told me."

"Penny's probably sitting in that police station, scared and crying, waiting for Daddy."

"I'm sure she is," Ma said," I wish he'd call me, but knowing him, he'll probably stop at the bar on the way home, just to torture Penny a little longer."

We waited and waited... and ran to the window with every car we heard. Finally, around 9 o'clock, they pulled in. Penny walked in dragging her little pink school bag behind her. Her red curls were in a tangled mess. She'd been crying and her face was all red and swollen.

"Now you get in there and sit on that bed without any supper," Daddy yelled, "and start thinking about what you're going to get when I get home." Daddy walked back outside, slammed the door, jumped in his car and left.

We ran in to see Penny. Ma took her a chicken wing and a piece of bread with butter. She put her arms around Penny. "You'll be okay. Here, eat this, then you can tell us what happened."

Penny sniffed and took a bite of chicken. "I just wanted to get everyone something nice, but I didn't have any money. Shelly told me that she goes in the store all the time and gets anything she wants. She just sneaks stuff in her school bag. She said it was easy. I told her I couldn't do that. If I got caught, Daddy would kill me. She said we wouldn't get caught, because it was foolproof."

"Well, you see how fool proof it was," Ma said.

"I do now," Penny said.

"Then what happened?" I asked.

"Shelly's mom dropped us off at the store. We both went a different way. I did what she told me and kept my eyes open for the security guard. I found the things I wanted and put them in my school bag. I was so nervous. My heart was beating fast, but I didn't think anyone saw me. And you guys liked all the stuff I got you last week."

"You told me you found that money." Ma said.

"I'm sorry." Penny started crying again, "but I lied."

"Well it's over now," Ma said. "I hope you learned your lesson. Now finish your story."

Penny blew her nose. "Just as I slipped the last thing in my bag I felt a hand on my shoulder. I was to scared to even turn around. The security guard walked in front of me."

"What do you have in your bag?" he asked.

"I couldn't even talk, I could barely breathe. I looked up and Shelly was walking beside a tall police woman, heading straight towards me. They put us both in the squad car and hauled us down to the police station. They asked a lot of questions, then locked us in a room behind a steel door with a small glass window. They said they were going to call our parents. I was praying that Daddy wouldn't pick me up. I wanted to stay with the nice police woman. I kept my eyes on the little window. Daddy walked up to the lady at the desk, then Shelly's dad came in. We watched them through the little window until they both turned and headed our way."

"Turn on the tears," Shelly said, "that will help."

"We did turn on the tears, but it didn't do anything for Daddy."

"Get out in this car!" he yelled, "and stop bawling. You can sit in the front seat with me, then I won't have to reach behind the seat, in case I want to hit you."

"Daddy pulled into the Cozy Corner Bar. He made me sit in the car by myself. And he left me sitting out there for over three hours. I kept seeing those teenage guys walking through the alley. They were smoking, swearing, and whistling at all the girls who walked by. I had to go to the bathroom. I was tired and hungry. Boy, this chicken tastes good."

DADDY NEVER CALLED ME PRINCESS

"So what was it that you stole?" Ma asked.

"I took a bottle of Tabu for you, Mama, and a jar of Noxzema for Wanda. A little red truck for Ronnie and a new box of crayons for Rodney, so he wouldn't have to use all those broken ones."

"What did you get for yourself?" Ma said.

"Nothing," Penny said. "I just wanted to make all of you happy with a small gift."

Ma started crying. She put her arms around Penny. "Would you like me to get you another chicken wing? Then you can go to sleep, you've been through a lot."

"Yeah," Penny said, "and I'll never forget this day. But I learned my lesson well. No more stealing for me. I won't even pick up a penny if I see one lying in the street."

CHAPTER 27:
GET A JOB

"In the confrontation between the river and the rock the river always wins...

not through strength, but by perseverance."

- Author unknown.

"Get a job?" Could a naive, sheltered teenage girl, who was afraid of her own shadow, ever expect to find a job? I didn't even drive, or have a car, and I knew Daddy wouldn't help.

Ma held out a little money from her grocery budget, bless her heart, and she gave it to me. So I had a little saved up to at least pay for a taxi, if I did find work. I wasn't sure where to start, I didn't have any experience. Maybe it would be best to do some volunteer work first. My school had a program called "Future Nurses," so I applied and they accepted me.

I had my little candy striper outfit on and it was my first night. I was a nervous wreck. Someone gave me a tour of the hospital then my first assignment was to go around to all the rooms and give the patients fresh ice water. In the first room a man was lying in bed watching television. I tried my best to act friendly as I gave him my best smile. I grabbed his pitcher and walked out of the room. I wanted to do a really good job so I filled it to the top with ice before adding the water. I walked back into his room and set the refill on his table.

DADDY NEVER CALLED ME PRINCESS

He started laughing. "Wow," he said, "that will be refreshing."

"I hope so," I said, "and I even gave you extra ice." I didn't find out until I left the room that I had not filled his ice pitcher, but his urinal.

I eventually learned to do better, but I had dreams of all the things I wanted to buy for my family, and I needed money, so my search for a part-time job began. The first place I applied was Aunt Nina's, as a carhop. The drive-in was only about a mile from home and they hired me on the spot. I was so nervous my first night. What if I messed up? I had never even traveled many miles away from home, and I didn't really have any social skills.

Aunt Nina's was a place where people pulled up, placed their orders through a speaker next to their car, and the carhops carried the orders out on a tray that hooked over the car window. When the diners finished, the carhops collected the trays and hopefully found a good tip lying there. I'd somehow managed my first few orders, when a man asked me a question.

"Do you have breaded shrimp?"

I had no clue, I'd never tasted shrimp, and didn't even know what breaded shrimp was.

"I don't know," I said, "but I'll go ask." So I fearfully went inside to find the manager.

"Some man wants to know," I asked him, "do you breed your shrimp?"

He looked at me like I was crazy. Maybe he thought the man was pulling my leg.

"No," he said, "we don't."

Somehow, I made it through my first night. I was so excited to feel my apron weighed down with silver at the end of my shift. At closing time I ordered food to go. The taxi driver took me home. Everyone met me at the door. "What smells so good?" Ma wanted to know.

GET A JOB

"Coneys and fries," I said, "I brought some for everyone, and even milkshakes." Penny dipped fries in her chocolate shake, the boys did the same as they all laughed. Ma loved her Coney Island. After we finished eating I took my apron off and dumped all my quarters, dimes, and nickels on the table. We counted it together and I still had over ten dollars left.

When I went back to work the next night it was 90 degrees. I was carrying a man's order for half a dozen Cokes, with lots of ice. As I tried to hook the tray over his window something got caught, the tray tipped, the covers popped off, and he got a seat full. He yelled and jumped out of the car brushing ice off his lap.

"Wow," he said, "that really cooled me off."

"Oh, I'm so sorry," I told him, "I'll get you another order." But he managed to laugh about it and tried to make me feel better by telling me that it could happen to anyone.

"Just make it 'to go' this time," he said, "and not so much ice."

I went back inside to pick up his order. "Hey, Wanda," the manager yelled, "you have an emergency phone call from your mother." Ma knew she wasn't supposed to call me at work, but that never stopped her. The big emergency was that she only wanted light onions on her Coney.

"Ma, you're going to get me fired. I'm not supposed to talk on the phone now."

"Oh, I told them it was an emergency," she said, "they don't know any better. If they fire you, so what, there are always other jobs out there."

But I kept working and I was able to save a little money. I had plans to buy my brothers and sister, one at a time, their first bike. I wanted to surprise Ma with something she really needed, a couch. The only thing she owned was her home-made sectional. The cement blocks were still under the corners holding it up, and she still covered it with a blanket. The old thing was looking pretty rough and it hardly provided any support. The taxi driver took me

DADDY NEVER CALLED ME PRINCESS

to the nearest furniture store. After looking around the clearance center I spotted a cocoa brown couch. "How much are you asking for that couch?" I said.

"You can have it for $50," he said.

"Sold."

They even agreed to deliver it for free. Ma had tears in her eyes when the truck pulled in and she saw her surprise sofa. "Look, Ma," I said, "you don't even have to keep it under wraps."

But she covered it anyway. "To protect it," she said.

The boss finally tired of all my emergency calls and I had to look for another job.

"Don't worry," Ma said. "I had lots of jobs at your age, you'll find another one." My next job was working in a bakery, all inside work, and it was great. One of my jobs was to fill the doughnuts. My favorites were the cream-sticks. The white cream oozed out the ends when I finished. Closing time I was given left-over doughnuts, bags full, every night. Nutty doughnuts, glazed, bis-marks, sugar-coated, I didn't know there were so many different kinds to devour. They also filled orders for beautifully decorated cakes. There were half a dozen cakes on a tray, just waiting for boxes. The boss told me to carry the tray of cakes to the back room so they could be ready for pick up. The cakes certainly looked heavy and I wasn't too strong. I didn't think I could carry them all at once and I told the boss so.

"Sure you can," he said, "just be careful and don't drop them."

I reached under the tray on both ends and tried to lift them but the cakes started sliding. Try as I might I couldn't hold them. SPLAT! I saw picture-stopping cakes strewn all over the floor. "Happy Birthday John" in blue on thick white icing, "Happy Anniversary Mom & Dad" garnished with perfect little red roses, and other beautiful cakes in a smashed-up glob. I resigned myself to looking for another job. I wasn't strong enough to handle that one.

GET A JOB

The taxi cab driver, John, considered me one of his regulars. I felt safe riding the back roads with him in the driver's seat. "So, Wanda," he'd ask, "where are we working tonight?"

My next job was waiting tables in a diner and I was in training. "Always take a glass of water and a menu when you walk over to the table. Smile and be friendly. If they have children, offer to get them a highchair. After they've had a couple bites of their food go back to the table and ask them how it tastes. The customer is always right." All the training paid off and I got larger tips. Sometimes even a whole dollar, and if they really liked my service, maybe two.

While working one night, everyone suddenly got quiet. All the help kept their focus on a man who was sitting alone, at one of my tables. I didn't know what was happening, but the manager called me over and whispered. "Just go wait on him," he said, "like nothing is wrong. We have everything under control. The police were called."

I wondered why they needed the police, but I did what the manager told me. I walked up to the table with a glass of water, a menu and a smile. My smile almost froze when I looked in the booth beside him. Lying there, within reach of his hand, was a rifle. I pretended not to notice. I figured maybe if I was friendly then he wouldn't shoot me. I took his order, praying that I'd get it right, and walked back to the kitchen. Everyone was talking about him. He was the boyfriend of one of the girls who worked there. She had broken up with the rebel and he was on the rampage. He had told her that he was going to kill her if she didn't come back to him.

Thankfully, before his order was ready, the police came in quietly through the back entrance. They managed to talk to the guy, then they handcuffed him and took him out without any harm or gunfire. After Ma heard about that she didn't think it was safe for me to work there.

My next job was working as a cashier in the neighborhood grocery store. I really enjoyed my job and found out that I did well as a cashier. I kept that job for almost a year and a half. I didn't get

DADDY NEVER CALLED ME PRINCESS

any tips, but the pay was better than any I'd had before, and I was able to buy things.

The first one to get his bike was Ronnie. Watching him get excited over his green Schwinn with the basket on front was awesome. He rode around the neighborhood with the best of them. I could hardly wait to buy the next one. I also bought a small pool for everyone to share. Penny wanted white Go Go boots and a white dress, the boys wanted trucks and cars. "Oh, you're the best sister ever," the kids would say." Ma couldn't get enough Tabu cologne. I was glad they were happy, but I think I got more out of it than they did. I was thankful that I was able to buy stuff for them, and all because I conquered my fears and got a job.

CHAPTER 28:
LIFE, DEATH & EXES

"Do not pray for easy lives. Pray to be stronger men."

-John F. Kennedy

"You're pregnant?"

I was sixteen, Ronnie thirteen, Penny eleven, and Rodney, the youngest, was seven when Ma surprised us with the news that she was having another baby. I worried about Ma, because of her age. I didn't know other women had babies at thirty-nine. I also wondered how she'd deal with a little one again. Would we be fighting to hold her legs up? Would I have to keep an eye on her in case she had a nervous breakdown? But she didn't seem worried.

"I've been through it all before," she said, seeming to take everything in stride. Maybe, if Ma wasn't worried, then I didn't need to worry either. I could relax.

Ma had an easy pregnancy. Her feet did swell up. But she was able to buy a foot stool, instead of using us kids to hold her legs up. We still waited on her because we loved her. In fact, if I was down the road, visiting with the neighbor's, Ma would send one of the kids after me.

"Ma wants you to come home."

I'd walk home and more often than not, she'd say, "I just want

DADDY NEVER CALLED ME PRINCESS

you to close the drapes, you're tall." So I'd close the drapes, or thread the needle, or whatever else she wanted me to do.

The months passed, Ma grew larger, the big day finally arrived, I thought. She started having pains and called Daddy home. He took her to the hospital. Several hours later, they came home. Ma was still pregnant. She said it was false labor. Fours days later she was still having pains, but no baby. I was so worried about her, after all the horror stories I'd heard about having babies. The stories scared me so bad I didn't know if I ever wanted to have a baby. Then Ma started having stronger pains, and they lasted longer, so it was back to the hospital. She stayed that time. Several hours later, Daddy called and told us it was a girl, and that he'd be home later. I was so thankful to Jesus for helping Ma get her baby born safely.

I scrounged through the cupboards, trying to find something for supper. The only thing I came up with was pieces of bread, cooked on the stove, and sugar boiled down to make syrup. But the kids said it was delicious. I was too afraid to ask Daddy to take me to the store, so we just made do, with whatever we could find, mostly brown bananas, lettuce and day old bread. Several days later Ma came home with a precious little baby girl. Lots of bright red curly hair peeked out from under her tiny hat. Ma named her Rena. I'd rock my little sister in my arms and sing while feeding her the bottle. The fresh scent of baby powder was so sweet. I'd take one of my fingers and put it inside her little hand. She'd wrap her tiny fingers around my slim finger. Then I'd lay her in the bassinet, the soft flannel blanket next to her chubby cheek, and she'd fall asleep. She looked like a little doll. I couldn't get enough pictures. I did a lot of day dreaming, pretending Rena was mine. Having a baby in the house again brought a new kind of joy.

Ma would sing songs and talk to her. Before we knew it Rena was almost 5 months old. She showed a real interest in all the family. She would laugh and squeal with delight. Ma said with all her endearing babble, she showed promise of being a real talker someday. Little Rena gave us a new reason to get up in the morning and another birthday to celebrate.

LIFE, DEATH & EXES

We had just celebrated Penny's 12th birthday with cake and ice cream. Ma wanted to get away from the house for a while and Daddy planned to take her to town. They asked Penny if she wanted to go along, since it was her birthday. I stayed home and baby-sat, got the kids settled for the night, then climbed into bed and fell sound asleep.

I woke up when I heard the door slam and Daddy yelling for Ma to cook his steak. Penny came and got into bed beside me.

"So, how was your birthday outing?" I whispered.

"Some outing," she said. "Daddy stopped at the bar for a quick one. He left me sitting in the car alone. One of Daddy's friends pulled in the parking lot and walked over to the car.

"Aren't you hot out here?" he asked.

I told him I was fine, but he insisted that I go into the bar with him.

"No," I said, "Daddy will be mad."

"Don't worry about your dad," he said, "I'll take care of him."

So I went in the bar with him. "Hey, Lyle, what do you mean leaving this little girl out in the car by herself? She's burning up out there."

Daddy reached in his pocket. "Here's some money," he told me, "you can walk next door and buy yourself a hot dog for your birthday."

He gave me three dollars. I took the money and walked over to the diner. I climbed up on one of the red bar stools. My feet didn't even reach the floor. I wasn't sure if I'd have enough money for a drink too, so I just ordered a hot dog. Then I sang "Happy Birthday to me," in my mind while I ate my hot dog, hoping I'd have enough money. When the waitress gave me the check I was glad to see that I could pay the bill. I had enough money to leave a tip, and even some birthday change left over. I climbed down off the stool and walked back next door. But when I walked into the bar, Daddy held

DADDY NEVER CALLED ME PRINCESS

out his hand.

"Okay," he said, "give me back my change."

"You're kidding?" I said.

"Nope." Then Penny gave a deep sigh and fell asleep.

"Well that figures," I whispered as I felt myself dozing off.

We woke up in the morning to the usual sounds of Ma cleaning the house. Shaking rugs, vacuuming, dusting. She was a perfectionist. She kept our meager house spotless. Even though the wood floors were never finished, Ma had waxed them so much they always sparkled. She hung pictures all over the walls, even before they were dry walled. She liked everything neat and tidy. We learned not to leave things lying around, or they'd disappear in short order, like all my magazines.

I spent a lot of time reading Modern Romance magazines. I came home one day and all my magazines were gone. Ma had thrown them in the garbage while I was at school. She made me so mad. "Why did you do that?" I asked her. "I had money hidden inside one of them."

"Too bad," she said, "maybe next time you won't leave them lying all over the house."

I spent a lot of time reading, day dreaming and wondering if I'd ever get another boyfriend that I loved as much as Lucky. Then I got a pleasant surprise, even better, and my heart did flip-flops. Lucky called. He wanted to see me. We started going out again and he even had a car. He took me to meet his parents, we went out to eat, and sometimes we just drove around. I had to meet him in secret because Daddy didn't know Lucky was back in my life. I still made sure I was home before the bars closed. But I was almost eighteen and ready to fight Daddy for the love of my life. All Lucky had to do was ask. But he didn't ask, and things were never the same. Something was wrong. Like the old song goes, "How can you tell if he loves you so? It's in His Kiss." Well, it wasn't. I felt like something was not quite right, from the beginning, but I didn't want

LIFE, DEATH & EXES

to believe it. My heart longed for the closeness that we used to share, but instead, I felt the aloofness when he took me in his arms. He still looked the same, he still wore the same aftershave, but he acted different. He didn't hold me as tight as he used to. When he kissed me, nothing felt right. Several weeks later, things were still cool between us, even though he told me he loved me. I couldn't go on living in limbo.

I called Lucky one evening. I had to know how he felt. Did he still love me?

I was crying.

"Lucky?" I sniffed, "Lucky?"

He didn't answer. That said it all. He silently hung up and I knew it was over between us.

My heart was broken, a second time, by my first love. I was careful not to cry in front of Daddy. If he ever found out that Lucky and I were back together that summer, he would have kicked me out of the house. And I couldn't afford to live anywhere else. My last year of high school was just beginning, and it was a shocker.

I was sitting in Econ class when word came over the loudspeakers.

"President Kennedy's been shot."

Talking stopped and an instant hush came over the room. Some people were crying. Someone brought in a television and we watched in silent horror. We had studied about Abe Lincoln, but this was now and it was happening during out lifetime. School let out and everyone boarded the bus in shocked silence. The usual rowdy, noisy crowd was as somber as if marching to our own death.

I climbed off the bus, ran into the house and told Ma.

"President Kennedy's been shot and he's dead!"

"Oh, I'm sure," Ma said.

"Well turn on the television," I told her. We spent the rest of

143

DADDY NEVER CALLED ME PRINCESS

the evening watching as everything else unfolded and our country changed forever.

Life was full of changes during my senior year. I could only imagine what other things life had in store for me.

CHAPTER 29:
SENIOR TEARS

"Use what talents you possess. The woods would be very silent if no birds sang there, except those that sang best."

- Author unknown

Senior year. The year of 'lasts.'

Another chapter of my life was about to close. Some people told me it would be the best year of my life. So far, I could only hope that wasn't true. Someone else said, "Remember: It's not the end, it's the beginning." I liked that better.

No more taking notes to the dean, with all the lies explaining why I had missed so much school. The dean knew they were mostly lies, but Ma always wrote the notes. How could the gruff woman, with the tight bun, who sat behind her big desk and glared at me through thick glasses, ever question my mother?

I had saved up enough money for my senior portraits and could hardly wait to have them taken. I never thought I was pretty, but the photographer was known to make anyone look good. I was pleasantly surprised when I got the proofs. One of the girls looked at my picture and said,

"Cow a Bunga."

There was also enough money left to rent my cap and gown and order a yearbook. But the one thing I still wanted was my class ring, and everyone was getting measured for theirs. Seniors looked at the

DADDY NEVER CALLED ME PRINCESS

catalogs and tried to decide which ring they liked best. Girls couldn't wait until their boyfriends ordered, they knew they'd be wearing the ring soon enough.

"Hey, Wanda," people asked, "what kind of ring are you going to order?"

"Oh, I haven't decided yet."

All of them were pretty, but my favorite ring had the name of our school in gold, and a blue stone in the back, since our colors were blue and gold. The simple ring that I liked cost $25, and I dared not even hope that I'd have enough money to order one.

Ma knew how much I wanted a ring, but she didn't have that kind of money either. And we all knew that Daddy exchanged most of his money at the corner bar.

I came home from school a few days later and Ma was all smiles, like a kid on Christmas morning. "I talked to your dad," she said, "and he wanted me to give you something."

She handed me an envelope. I opened it and there was $25 inside.

"Well what's this for?" I asked.

"He wants you to buy your class ring."

I was so shocked and happy that I started bawling. My daddy showed a little love, after all, and that meant more than the ring itself. I would cherish it forever.

When my ring came in I wore it proudly, putting my hand out and showing it off, just like everyone else. They didn't know how much that ring really meant to me. It was a sign that maybe daddy really did love me. He had parted with some of his drinking money, just for me.

I didn't have any plans for college. A couple of big things stood in my way. Number one, there was no money available for tuition. Number two, even though I was graduating, it certainly wasn't

SENIOR TEARS

because I had good grades. Valedictorian I was not. Since I rarely showed up at school, I fit right in among the lower end of the class, with barely passing grades. But still, I was passing.

Others were preparing for college, some were planning, or had to get married. I was just taking it one day at a time. But the only thing I ever really wanted to do was fall in love, get married and have five kids. There's nothing I wanted more.

I busied myself, preparing for graduation. I had been in choir for the past four years and we were singing for the graduation service. But before I could receive my diploma I had to show my birth certificate, which I didn't have, so I wrote a letter asking for a copy. When I received a copy the name of my real dad showed as my last name. When I showed my birth certificate to the dean she questioned my last name. "That's not the name," she said, "that you went by for the past thirteen years."

"I know, I've gone by the name of the man who raised me all these years, and I want his name on my diploma. Not the name I was given at birth, that's the name of my real dad, but I don't even know him."

"Well, I'm sorry," she said, "but the name on your birth certificate will be the name that goes on your diploma."

Then this quiet little girl, who never said boo to anyone, stood tall beside the school dean and argued for all she was worth.

"You can't do that!" I said. "The man who raised me is the only dad I ever knew. He paid for my education and if I walk across that stage and you call out the name of my real dad, it will break his heart. I won't do that to him. You have to put his name on my diploma."

"I'm sorry," she said again, "but we have rules and I can't change them for you."

I stood my ground until she finally agreed that she'd see what she could do.

DADDY NEVER CALLED ME PRINCESS

Graduation day finally arrived. I still wasn't sure whose name they were going to call out when I walked across the stage, but I prayed that it would be daddy's last name. My classmates had people coming from all over to watch them graduate.

Pomp and Circumstance. The Graduation March started to play, "Land of Hope and Glory." The seniors marched up the aisle by twos, most of the girls taking the arms of the guys. Tassels on the right side of our caps were gently swaying. I tried scanning the crowd, looking for anyone in the family, but especially Ma and Daddy. I couldn't find even one familiar face to watch me receive my diploma. That really didn't surprise me, neither one of them had come to any school function I'd ever had. But I still had hopes that they'd at least be there for my graduation.

I took my place on stage with the choir, getting ready to sing the Hallelujah Chorus. I was so disappointed. I tried to ignore the pain and focus on graduation, but I didn't even know if I'd be able to sing. The band started and voices boomed out, except mine, I could only mouth the words and choke back tears.

About half way through the song I noticed some commotion in the back of the room. I glanced that way and Ma and Daddy were walking up the aisle. They were both drunk, and they came late, but I wasn't even mad about that. They both cared enough to show up and I was thrilled to the core of my being. The next words of the song, which I managed to sing, fit perfectly.

"And He shall reign forever and ever, King of kings! And Lord of lords!"

I would proudly walk across that stage and move my tassel from the right to the left side, and begin a whole new life. "But please," I kept praying, "let them call Daddy's name when they call me." Because the dean had only promised to try, she never said for sure.

We sat in that warm auditorium and listened to all the speakers evoke emotions from everyone. We waited patiently for our turn to walk across that stage for the last time. Roll call began. They eventually called my name, "Wanda," and I held my breath until I

SENIOR TEARS

heard Daddy's last name. After breathing a huge sigh of relief, my legs turned to rubber and my body started to shake. I somehow managed to walk cross the stage, wiping tears, and receive my diploma.

My classmates didn't have to wonder why they called me by a different name. They called me by the name they'd known me by for the past thirteen years. I didn't have to explain. But I knew I only made it that far because of Daddy. He had pushed me to keep in school, Ma wouldn't have minded if I had quit. But bless her heart, she just never thought it was that important, especially since all I ever wanted to do was get married and have a family.

When graduation was over all my friends headed out to party. I went home with Ma and Daddy. I got something to eat, then went into my room just as Ma was coming out. She'd been looking at my yearbook. Many people had signed it but when I looked again I found a new signature inside. Ma had taken a full-page and wrote a letter. Here's what she wrote.

To a girl I remember from a wee little pumpkin, who I nursed through measles, chicken pox, etc., who I watched grow up into a very beautiful young lady, who went out on dates & told me all her happiness & troubles, who I watched so proud & happy to receive her diploma & to you, Wanda, I wish all the Happiness & Luck in the world. From someone who knows & Loves you very, very much. "Guess who?"   Mother

Sitting down on the bed I started to cry. She'd had a hard life. Her kids were always her reason for living. I wanted to find a way to help her, somehow.

Senior year was not my best year. But I had hopes of better things ahead. I was going to work full-time at Aunt Nina's. I planned to save some money, buy a car, and get my own apartment. Then Ma, along with my brothers and sisters, could come & live with me. Ma would finally have a way out, if she wanted it. Maybe I could even start a hope chest in preparation for my own wedding, someday in the future.

CHAPTER 30:
RIGHT OR WRONG

"This just didn't happen to girls like me. This just didn't happen to anyone."

- Jenna-Lynne Duncan, Hurricane

    I was seventeen years old, recently graduated, and back working at Aunt Nina's full-time. Lucky was out of my life, again. There was always some guy hanging out where I worked. They'd order a little at a time, so they'd have more time to talk with the carhops. Some guys acted interested, but I knew what they really wanted, so I wasn't. Until Tim.

    The new guy in town. Tall, wavy blond hair, baby blue eyes, what a catch. He worked for the local Tree Trimming company. Tim came around a lot. He kept watching me. Then one day, I couldn't believe it, he asked me out. He reminded me of Lucky, a real gentleman. I said "Yes." He was going to pick me up after work. I called Ma and told her I'd be home late.

    Tim pulled up just before we closed. When my shift was over it was time for me to mop the floor, but one of the guys offered to do it for me. I thanked him, wrapped up my apron full of change, threw it in a bag, grabbed my purse and left. I climbed into the car with Tim.

    "What time do you have to be home?" he asked.

    "Oh, just as long as I'm home before the bars close," I said, not

DADDY NEVER CALLED ME PRINCESS

even realizing that guys would take it the wrong way.

We rode around for awhile, just talking and laughing. Then we went back to Aunt Nina's to get something to eat. That seemed weird, I didn't have to serve the order. Tim was a few years older than me and a very interesting guy. He'd been in the service and had been honorably discharged. I highly respected him for serving our country.

We left Aunt Nina's and went to a restaurant where they allowed dancing.

"I've never danced before," I told him when he asked. "I don't even know how."

"Oh, it's easy," he said," just follow my lead. I'll teach you."

He sauntered over to the jukebox box, put a quarter in, and I heard his song. "Right or Wrong." (I'll be with you.) for the first time. "If you will say you love me, my life with you I'll share. Won't you take me along, to be with you right or wrong?"

He came back to the table and held his hands out. I followed him out to the dance floor. He took me in his arms and pulled me tight. "Just follow my rhythm," he said.

Swaying around the dance floor in his arms was great, and I fell in love with dancing. He told me I was pretty and he made me feel special. He wanted to know all about me. He was easy to talk to and I even found myself telling him about Daddy's abuse. He said he was so sorry for all that I'd been through. We danced, talked and laughed the night away. But I knew if I wanted to make it home before Daddy we'd have to leave. On the way home he pulled the car off to the side of a country road and cut the lights. He kissed me, a real kiss, just like in the movies. Cloud nine flew past, I was on cloud twenty.

"Have you ever been with a man?" he asked.

Oh, no, I thought, here it comes, he's just like all the other guys.

"Well, no," I told him, "why are you asking me that?"

RIGHT OR WRONG

"Because I love you," he said, "will you marry me? I want to be your first."

That put me in shock. "This is too fast," I said, "we hardly know one another."

"But I'll take you away from all the abuse, I can make you happy. Will you just think about it?"

Getting a marriage proposal was so exciting. I only thought of marriage as something far, far, into the future. I couldn't leave Ma and my brothers and sisters alone. But I told him I'd think about it.

He took me home and walked me to the door. There was a full moon and it was like I'd never seen it before. He took me in his arms and kissed me goodnight.

"You look so gorgeous," he said, "with the moon shining behind your face. Whenever I look at the moon I'll be thinking of you."

I floated into the house, all excited to tell Ma about my proposal.

Ma always stayed awake till I got home, then she wanted me to sit on her bed and tell her all about my date. "Are you awake, Ma?"

"Yeah, sweetie, come on in. Did you have a good time?"

"I had a wonderful time. You'll never guess what happened? He asked me to marry him."

"Well," she asked, "do you love him?"

"Well, I don't know, I just met him. But he's older and more mature. I do feel different about him than I've ever felt about anyone else."

"If you love him," she said, "then don't let him get away. You never forget your first love. I never did. And if you lose him, like you lost Lucky, you'll regret it for the rest of your life."

I didn't want to live the rest of my life pining over a lost love, but first, we'd have to spend time getting to know each other. We

DADDY NEVER CALLED ME PRINCESS

wouldn't tell Daddy we were even thinking about marriage, but only that we were dating.

When I brought Tim home, Daddy didn't like him at all, he though he was too cocky.

Time passed. Tim picked me up every night after work. We had fun. I liked him more every day. He was a perfect gentleman and never tried to push me past where I wanted to go.

I was about to turn eighteen, no longer under Daddy's control. Tim called the night before my birthday. He wanted to take me to meet his parents. Daddy was home that night, so I told Tim he'd have to ask him. Tim came over, he put on a pretty good show for Daddy, and got permission for me to go meet his parents.

I jumped into the car with Tim and waved good-bye to my family.

Tim kept driving and driving until I finally asked, "Where do your parents live?"

"In Illinois," he said.

I started to panic. "Well, I can't go to Illinois. That's over 500 miles away."

"We plan on being married anyway," he said, "we'll just elope."

"Well I'm not ready. We've talked about marriage, but I don't want to elope. I want to have a wedding with all my family there. I don't even have a suitcase, or any clothes, except what's on my back."

"That's okay," he said, "I'll buy you all new clothes. Besides, after we get married, you won't need any."

I tried to convince him to stop and let me call home, but he refused. He just kept driving. He finally had to pull in for gas. I needed to use the restroom and figured I could make a call when I went after the key. But he was right behind me and wouldn't let me call. I was getting really scared, but we had been thinking about

RIGHT OR WRONG

marriage, this would just be a little sooner than planned. And I had been gone so long already, if I went back then, Daddy would kill me. Still, I didn't want to worry Ma, but Tim wouldn't let me near a phone.

Later, we stopped to get something to eat and went inside. Tim grabbed my hand and pulled me over to the jukebox. He put in a quarter and played, "Right Or Wrong."

"Listen, honey," he said. "They're playing our song."

"Our song? We have a song?" And it was kind of nice; maybe this wouldn't be so bad.

After driving many long hours he pulled into a little town called Rock Falls. He pounded on the door and got his family out of bed. He introduced me to everyone as his bride-to-be. They all seemed really nice, especially his mom. She reminded me of my own. I was so sleepy, and gladly accepted the offer to crawl into bed with Tim's little sister for the rest of the night. I fell asleep wondering how my family was doing back home.

The next day Tim told his mother to plan our wedding, and she eagerly agreed. The family scrounged around and found some clothes that would fit me. I wondered if I should tell his mom that he'd kidnapped me, but she seemed so happy, and I didn't want to tell her bad things about her son. If only I could call Ma and find out what was going on back home.

Tim finally agreed to let me call, but he had a hold on my arm and told me what to say.

"Just tell them you're fine, we're going to get married, and we'll be living in Illinois."

I didn't like the sound of that, I just wanted to go home, but I agreed so he'd let me call.

When I finally got Ma on the phone she started crying. I convinced her that I was fine, but that I missed everyone. I didn't mention the fact that he took me by force.

DADDY NEVER CALLED ME PRINCESS

"Well, you can't come back here," she said. "Your dad is so mad and he called the police. They told him that as long as you were eighteen there's nothing they could do about it. So he had a fit and said he was going to get his gun and hunt you down. He said he'd shoot all the tires off Tim's car first, then he'd go after him. He took all of your clothes and put them outside in a pile to set on fire. He took all your pictures, even your graduation picture, and broke them all to pieces. He's so mad. You'd better keep away from here for awhile."

So I told her not to worry about me. I was happy, we were going to get married and live in Illinois.

Tim's mom did everything to plan a small, but nice wedding for us. She even took me out and offered to buy me a wedding dress. "What kind of dress would you like?" she asked.

"I don't care," I told her, "just as long as it's white."

His mom planned it all while I followed her around. Tim spent most of his time sleeping on the couch.

The big day finally arrived. We were getting married in a church and Tim's little sister was my bride's maid. His mom had sent invitations and there were probably about fifty people sitting in church, all on the groom's side. Not a soul, from my side of the family. I walked down the aisle in my white dress, carrying a bouquet of red and white carnations, in complete silence. I was so sad because Ma wasn't there, or my brothers and sisters. And even if Daddy was abusive, somehow, I always thought he'd walk me down the aisle on my wedding day.

Tim had talked his parents into renting us a small two room apartment. It was waiting. They threw us a reception but Tim was in a big hurry to leave. I was so nervous about our wedding night. Tim told me that he was known as the greatest lover in Rock Falls. I naively wondered how I'd ever measure up. I'd never been with a man and didn't even know what to do.

Back at our apartment I was going to put on the pretty

RIGHT OR WRONG

nightgown that his mom had bought for me, but I didn't get a chance. My dress had several tiny buttons up the back. Tim was so impatient, he ripped the dress apart and most of the buttons flew off. He ordered me to do things to please him. Then it was over.

"That can't be what everyone gets so excited about," I thought, but Tim seemed happy.

I got up and walked to the bathroom, he saw the red on the sheets.

"Huh," he said, "you really were telling the truth."

When I came back he told me to put some clothes on. We went down to the pool hall.

I sat alone and watched him play far into the night. I fought to stay awake until we went home.

The next morning I made pancakes for breakfast, a first for me. Tim took one bite.

"Well what in the world do you call this garbage?" He walked over and threw them in the trash, then went over to his mom's for breakfast.

Tim didn't have a job. We lived off his parents. Tim always wrote up a big list, when it was time to buy groceries, then he'd tell me to go over and have his mom take me to the store. I was so embarrassed to tell her that she also had to pay for everything.

The following week-end Tim dressed up, fit to kill, and headed out the door.

"Where are you going?" I asked.

"If I wanted you to know where I was going," he said, "I'd tell you before I hit the door."

So I stayed home and read magazines until bedtime, then went to bed alone.

Around 3 o'clock Tim came home drunk.

DADDY NEVER CALLED ME PRINCESS

"Hey," he yelled as he jerked me out of bed, "who just ran out the back door?"

"What are you talking about?" I said, with as much force as I could muster up. "No one, I've been asleep."

"I saw them sneak off when I pulled up. Don't lie to me!"

I had brush rollers in my hair, held in by the little pink picks. Tim grabbed the rollers and ripped them out of my head. Then he slapped me hard, right across the face. The force of it almost knocked me down.

"How dare you?" I screamed, "I watched my dad beat on my mother for years, and NO MAN, will ever beat on me!" The look in Tim's eyes was pure shock and he walked away.

A few nights later the same scene played again. He dressed to the hilt and went out. He came home and accused me of sleeping with some man. He saw them run out the back door when he pulled in, he said. He knew better. He only accused me of the things he'd been doing.

Then he jerked me out of bed and started slapping me back and forth across the face again, only that time, when I screamed at him, he didn't stop. He just hit me again. Harder. He was too strong for me and I felt powerless. I was 500 miles away from home, married to a man just like Daddy. I felt so helpless and alone.

Among other things, the beatings continued every few days. Once he even jerked me out of bed into the hall and pushed me down the stairs. Thankfully, I only ended up with bruises. People told me they saw him out with other women. Whenever I'd ask him what he did while he was out, I always got the same answer. "If I wanted you to know what I did," he'd say, "I'd tell you when I walked in the door."

I simply couldn't take it any longer. I would not allow Tim to use his fist on my face for his stress relief. Ma had put up with Daddy's abuse for years, and I was not about to follow in her footsteps. I only prayed that I wasn't pregnant.

RIGHT OR WRONG

Up until that point, I hadn't told Ma anything about the abuse. I didn't want to worry her. But I called and told her that I wanted to come home for a visit, by myself.

"Your dad is still mad," she said, "and he won't let you come home. But I'll talk to your uncle Pete and aunt Barb. I'm sure they'll let you stay with them for a while. Call me back and let me know when you're on the way."

I sold everything I had received for our wedding. Someone bought it all for $12, the price of a bus ticket. On one of Tim's next outings, I left.

Facing a twelve hour bus ride gave me a lot of time to think. Ma was probably expecting a woman of the world to climb off the bus, not a skinny, bedraggled waif of a girl, who looked like she was starving, probably because she was. After spending all the money on a ticket, there was nothing left for food during the trip.

A lady was walking the aisles, carrying little pillows. I looked forward to resting my head on something comfy. The man sitting in front of me said, "Yes," when she asked him if he wanted one. When I heard her say, "That will be 25 cents, please," I knew I wouldn't be getting a pillow. I was just glad that he'd asked first, so I wouldn't be embarrassed by not even having a quarter. I wondered what would be waiting for me when I climbed off the bus.

But, no matter what I faced when I got back, it had to be better than what I was leaving behind. Right or Wrong.

CHAPTER 31:
UNCLE PETE

"You won't drown in your tears if you can learn to swim through them."

- Daniel Conjwayo

"Bus stop 8 o'clock!"

Those were the only words I managed to get out before the operator cut me off. I didn't have any money for a real phone call and I needed to get a message to Ma. So I called the operator and told her I needed to make a person to person call. The second I heard Ma's voice I blurted out "Bus stop 8 o'clock!" then click, we were cut off. I only hoped that Ma understood and would be there waiting when I got off the bus. I had nowhere else to go.

The trip was a long and tiring one, without any food, and I was starving when the bus pulled into the station. I hadn't seen, or rarely spoken to, any of my family for several months. I looked out the window and was so happy to see Ma and uncle Pete, my favorite uncle. In fact I secretly think that he was everyone's favorite uncle, brother, dad, neighbor, just because he was an all around great person. Tall, slim, gentle, and all the women thought he looked great in a cowboy hat, especially his wife, Barbara. He always had a smile for everyone.

No one ever heard uncle Pete say an unkind word about a soul. And I never heard one swear word pass his lips. I remember when he quit smoking. He carried a package of Life Savors in his pocket.

DADDY NEVER CALLED ME PRINCESS

Whenever he'd get the urge for a cigarette he'd reach for a piece of candy instead, then he'd offer all of us one. By the time we passed it around and it got back to him it was usually empty paper. He'd just smile.

The family would get together, if Daddy was out of town, and sometimes we'd all climb into uncle Pete's car and go shopping. During our mall walk we'd stop for a bathroom break. When uncle Pete came out he'd ask, "If corn is a vegetable, and a tomato is a fruit, then what's a pea?" I can still see him laughing as he'd say, "A relief."

Cashew nuts were something else that he loved. We'd follow him to the counter where he'd order a bag of hot cashews, then he'd share with all of us. That meant we'd get a taste of something we couldn't afford at home. Before long all he had left was an empty bag.

I've always loved butter, or rather margarine, we couldn't afford butter at home. But whenever we'd eat at uncle Pete's he'd say, "Here comes Wanda, put on another stick of butter."

All of our family would get together and play country music. One of my favorite things to do was listen to uncle Pete sing while he played along on his guitar. We'd listen for hours, thinking he sounded like Johnny Cash. One of my favorite songs was "Black Sheep" by Stonewall Jackson. Uncle Pete would play the song and dedicate it to me.

Ma liked to bake Popovers, sometimes she even filled them with banana cream pudding. I can still see uncle Pete sitting at our kitchen table devouring a few of those. I enjoyed watching him and decided that if I ever had a little boy I was going to name him Pete.

After visiting uncle Pete's house, whenever we'd leave, he'd stand on the porch and wave until we were out of sight. Oh, I have so many memories of him. But seeing him there, through the bus window, was certainly a sight for sore eyes. And I had missed Ma so much.

UNCLE PETE

I stepped off the bus and hurried into her open arms. I couldn't stop the sobbing.

"What's wrong sweetie?" Ma tenderly asked.

She told me later that she had expected me to climb off the bus looking like a woman of the world, wearing stunning jewelry, high heels and a fur coat. She wasn't expecting to see me, looking even slimmer than when I had left, with dark bags under my sad eyes.

"I'll tell you all about it later," I said.

"You're probably hungry," Ma said, "I'll buy you a hot dog. What would you like on it?"

"Anything," I said, "even a plain hot dog would be great."

We sat at a table while I inhaled the hot dog, then I unburdened my soul. They were both so comforting and glad that I had gotten away safely.

"Your dad won't let you come home so Pete & Barbara are going to take you in for now.

I'll talk to your dad, maybe he'll change his mind later."

If I couldn't be with my own ma then staying with uncle Pete and aunt Barb would be great. Uncle Pete put his arms around me, "You're going to be okay. You can stay with us. He's not going to hurt you anymore."

Since Daddy refused to let me come back home I couldn't think of a better place to go with a broken heart. Uncle Pete and aunt Barb were an excellent example of what marriage should be like. They respected one another, I never saw them argue, they had fun and showed love to each other. Aunt Barb said her husband never raised his voice to her. Yes, uncle Pete was truly one of a kind. Both of them helped me as I tried to heal. If I ever got married again I could only hope to find a man just like him.

Someone gave me the name of a lawyer and I filed for a divorce. Since I didn't have any money to pay for everything, a

DADDY NEVER CALLED ME PRINCESS

petition was filed so that Tim would have to pay for the divorce, on the grounds of extreme mental and physical cruelty. Soon thereafter my lawyer received a letter in the mail. Tim's mother had sent a check for the entire amount. As much as I hated the thoughts of getting a divorce at eighteen years old, I wanted to go ahead and get it over with. When I found out that Tim's mom was going to pay for it I was so relieved.

The relief was short lived. My lawyer called, after receiving a call from Tim's mother. Apparently Tim had gotten mad at her, she didn't say if it was because she had sent the check, or something else. But Tim beat her black & blue, his own mother, and she put a stop payment on the check. I could not even imagine anyone beating their own mother. It brought back memories of all the times we watched Ma get beat and my heart broke from missing her so much, along with my sister's and brother's. I wondered if I'd ever be able to go home again.

CHAPTER 32:
HOME AGAIN

"Be not angry that you cannot make others as you wish them to be, since you cannot make yourself as you wish to be."

- Thomas Kempis

"Your dad said you can come home."

I had mixed feelings when Ma told me what Daddy said. I certainly missed her and my sister's and brother's, and living with uncle Pete seemed like paradise. But I'd been there for several weeks and I didn't want to wear out my welcome. I packed up my things, uncle Pete took me home and dropped me off. Daddy knew I was coming and he met me at the door.

"So, you want to come back home," he said. "Well let me tell you a thing or two!"

His voice kept escalating with every word as he shook his fist in my face.

"Whenever you think you're going to run this house, just let me know, cause you ain't gonna do it! And if you think you're going to move back here and run around with other guys, just because you learned that thing is good for something besides to pee out of, you can forget that to! As long as you're under my roof, you'll do as I say. You'll get a job, then come home at night and behave yourself. No running around and no guys coming over here either!"

"Okay, I told him, that's fine," but inside I crumpled.

DADDY NEVER CALLED ME PRINCESS

I found a job at Lee's grocery store as a cashier and I liked the work. Things back at home weren't any better between Ma and Daddy, they were getting worse. There were even times he didn't come home all night. He told Ma he was working out of town, doing odd electrical jobs to earn extra money. If so, we never saw any extra income.

But then his out of town trips came to a halt. Daddy needed to have surgery on his feet for Plantar warts. One of his friends drove him home after the surgery and helped him into bed. Ma took care of him and waited on him as best as she could. We knew that at least he wouldn't be going to the bars for awhile. But, after not too many days, Daddy finagled his way out of bed and drug himself into the living room. "What are you doing out of bed?" Ma asked him.

"I just want to run up to the Cozy Corner," he said.

Then he crawled outside on his hands and knees. He pulled himself up into the car, threw a pair of crutches in the backseat and away he went. He didn't return until the bars closed.

Something was driving Daddy, he just couldn't keep away from the bars or the booze. Then Ma told us another story about something that happened to him, years ago, before he started drinking. He was driving around, one dark night, when suddenly two boys on bikes came out of nowhere. Neither one of them had any lights and they were wearing dark clothing. He didn't spot them in his headlights until the last second and it was too late to stop. He hit the boys. It was just an accident, and it wasn't his fault, but they were both killed. I couldn't imagine how a person would be able to live with themselves, knowing they took the life of not only one, but two teenagers. I never knew how he was dealing with it because he refused to talk about the accident. In fact, he never talked to us kids about anything, unless it was something negative. Like the lock box he kept in his desk and dared anyone of us to touch it. We all wondered what he kept in there. Did he have another stash of food? Was he hiding money? He always had the key with him and we knew better than to break into his private metal treasure.

HOME AGAIN

Time passed and Daddy was back to normal, at least physically. He kept staying away for longer periods. Someone came and told Ma that Daddy was seeing another woman and living with her on the sly. I don't think she was too surprised. "Why don't you leave him?" I asked. "All he ever does is hurt you."

"Well it's not that easy," she said, "I don't have any money, or a place for all of us to live. I don't have any skills to get a job. I can't drive, and even if I could I don't have a car."

"Why don't you get a lawyer and make him pay," I said.

"That takes money too," she said. "I'm trapped."

So life went on, and somehow, we all kept going.

Ma never got much money from Daddy, as usual. But he never lacked for anything. In fact, he was driving a brand new 1965 Buick Wildcat. He came home the day he bought it and wanted to take all of us for a ride, just to show it off. There was a fresh car smell, everything sparkled and Ronnie said he sure know how to handle it. And Daddy still expected Ma to handle the house on what little he gave her, but it was never enough to keep up with the rising prices.

So I gave Ma the money I earned, and Ronnie decided that he wanted to get a job too. He wanted to help out and he was only 16 years old. Ma signed and gave him permission to quit school. I convinced my boss to hire him on as a stock boy. He worked in the store with me. Ronnie had his hours all figured out for his first pay check and he knew exactly what he was supposed to get. But when he got his check it was short.

"This isn't right," he complained.

I looked at his pay stub and found out he was only short because they had held out 46 cents for Old Age Benefit and 1 cent for city tax. He had worked for 18 ¾ hours and he brought home $12.31. So I explained to him the facts of life about taxes.

"Well that's not fair!" he said, "I worked for that. How can someone else just take my money without even asking?"

DADDY NEVER CALLED ME PRINCESS

"That's life," I told him, "just wait until you buy a house."

Penny wanted to get a job as a car hop at the Varsity Drive In. She was only 14, but with make-up, one of my outfits, and a big lie about her age, they hired her. Fourteen wasn't old enough to quit school either, so she only worked part time. On the days she worked, she skipped school. No one missed her, the Principal never even called.

And Daddy wasn't around long enough to even notice all the changes. We wondered if he'd ever be home again, we all hoped that he wouldn't, except for Ma. For some reason that we couldn't figure out, she missed him.

CHAPTER 33:
THE STRANGER

"We sometimes encounter people, even perfect strangers, who begin to interest us at first sight, somehow suddenly, all at once, before a word has been spoken.

- Fyodor Dostoevsky

A strange car pulled in the drive. Ma and all of us kids were sitting under the maple tree, too far away from the house to run. "You kids get over here by me," Ma said. A big, stocky man, well over six feet tall, climbed out of the car and headed straight towards us. As he walked closer Ma seemed to recognize him and she smiled.

"Is that you, Reta?" he asked.

"Bill," she said. "Wanda, that's your dad."

My dad, I thought, the man I've been hearing about all these years? The man who was so mean to Ma? She didn't act the least bit afraid. She stood up, walked over to him and they embraced.

Then Ma turned to me. "And this is Wanda."

I had any number of reasons to be mad at him: like walking away from us when I was little, for never trying to find me later in life, for all the times he hurt Ma and broke her heart.

But it all happened so fast that day. I didn't have time to think. He came over and stood in front of me. Then, for the first time I ever remembered, my dad's arms were around me. The anger left,

DADDY NEVER CALLED ME PRINCESS

for a moment. I finally felt a connection, and it was nice.

He had a head full of thick, wavy, gray hair. As he stood there I noticed his big feet and how they turned in, just a little, exactly like mine. I'd always wondered where I got that from. Ma never told me. I had a lot of questions. There were so many things I wanted to ask him: like why he never wanted me, or why didn't he love me. But they kept talking, so mostly all I did was listen.

I was surprised, after the way Ma had talked about him all those years, but they laughed and talked over old times like nothing had ever been wrong.

"We used to live in some awful places, didn't we, Reta?"

"That's for sure, how could I ever forget?"

"But you have to admit," he said, "we filled the rooms with lots of love."

Ma just smiled and nodded. Her blue eyes sparkled like they hadn't in a long time.

"Remember, Reta, when all we had to eat for days was an apple?"

"Yeah, I remember," she said with a laugh.

When he turned around and talked to the other kids, Ma whispered to me. "Don't leave me alone with him." And I knew it wasn't because she was afraid of him.

So I only went in the house once. I fixed some peanut butter and jelly sandwiches, along with some Kool-Aid for us kids. I made sure to grab my camera on the way out.

After setting the food on the picnic table, I stood in from of my parents. "Smile," I said, then I took the first and only picture of Ma and my real dad together, their arms around one another, each of them holding a can of beer.

While eating, I enjoyed listening to them talk.

Ma and Bill weren't hungry, they were too busy talking, sharing their lives, and the six-pack he'd brought.

Bill had a love for writing. He repeated some of his poems to us.

"How do you come up with those?" I asked.

"Well," he said, "I usually come up with them right off the top of my head."

"Let's see you do it," Ronnie said.

Bill was wearing the clothes he'd been painting in so Ronnie asked him to make up something about them. And true to his word, he came up with a poem in no time, and it fit perfectly. He gave me a copy of some of his writing's, and I kept all of them. They allowed me to have a small look into his soul. Some of his poems talked about his relationship with the Lord. I never realized, until years later, that his words would bring me such comfort.

I found out some other pleasantly surprising news. I had other brother's and at least one more sister. Bill told us a little about each of them. He said I looked just like my other sister.

Bill talked about his sister, Rosie. He was living with her at the time.

We sat outside and visited all afternoon. The other kids ran off to play, but I just sat there watching and listening, until the sun started to go down.

Bill was getting ready to leave. He gave Ma a good bye hug. Then he turned to me.

"You wouldn't happen to have a couple of bucks I could borrow for a six-pack, would you?"

It hurt me that he asked. But I went into the house, brought back $3.00 and gave it to him.

"Thanks, Wanda," he said, "and if you ever need anything, just let me know."

He hugged me, kissed me on the cheek, and said good-bye to

DADDY NEVER CALLED ME PRINCESS

everyone else.

Then, as fast as he came, he was gone.

I didn't know if I'd ever see or hear from him again, and I could probably kiss my $3.00 goodbye. But, at least for once in my life, I knew what it was like to be hugged by my dad, the stranger.

CHAPTER 34:
NEW BEGINNINGS

"The secret to a rich life is to have more beginnings than endings."

- Dave Weinbaum

With my job as a cashier over for the day, I had walked to the nearest restaurant. The bar stool just inside the door looked inviting, so I went in and sat down to rest my tired, aching feet. I ordered a Cherry Coke and sat at the counter, drinking and dreaming. Someone spoke to me.

"Hi, I'm Don."

I turned to look. He was not what you'd call handsome. He was a little overweight, had dark hair combed straight back, wore thick, large black glasses and was very casually dressed. I was lonely for someone to talk to. It had been over a year since my divorce, and he looked harmless. We started talking. He seemed very friendly and it was fun.

I could just be myself and I felt comfortable with him. I found out that we lived within a mile of each other, but he was ten years older that I was, and we'd never met. He had never been married. Before I knew it five hours had passed. I called a taxi to take me home and made plans with Don to meet again.

We became fast friends. He was very sympathetic and listened patiently, over time, while I told him about my life, including all the abuse I'd been through. Before long, I took Don home to meet all

DADDY NEVER CALLED ME PRINCESS

of my family, except Daddy. We didn't want him to know about my new boyfriend. Ma and my sisters and brothers all liked Don.

Then I went to meet all of his family. We didn't have far to go. "Hey, Don," they said, "how can a homely guy like you get such a pretty woman?" It was embarrassing to listen to all their wise cracks.

Several months went by and things were getting serious. Ma had a talk with Daddy. "If you keep her tied down too much she's just going to run off again." She convinced him to let me start dating so I took Don home to meet Daddy.

"Where did she meet that stupid idiot?" he asked Ma, later. Daddy wasn't too impressed.

Don and I continued to date. We were driving around one evening, about dusk. Don told me he could see just fine, even though he was squinting, and not wearing his glasses. Suddenly the person behind us laid on their horn, trying to get us to pull over. We discovered that it was Don's sister so he pulled to the side of the road. She ran up to the car and started yelling at him.

"Why are you driving without your glasses?" she said. "You know you can't see to drive without them, especially this time of night! Put them back on right now!"

Don must have been so embarrassed when she yelled at him in front of me. His face looked like a kid who knocked over the communion. He lit into her, up one side and down the other. He screamed right back and cuss words rolled off his tongue with ease.

She bent down, leaned in the window towards me and said, "Someday, that will be you."

I didn't believe her because I knew he'd never talk to me that way. Don put his glasses on and we drove away.

We'd been dating almost a year when Don started hinting around about getting married. I talked to Ma. "I think he's going to ask me to marry him."

"Oh," she said, "Don would make a good husband. He'd never

hurt you. He worships the ground you walk on. You're always worried about your hair, well he loves you so much that he wouldn't even care if you were bald-headed. He treats you like a queen. And you can trust him. You'd never have to worry about him wanting any other woman, the way your dad worries me. My heart aches just thinking about him with a girlfriend."

It would be nice, I thought, not having to worry about another man hurting me. I'd always felt so comfortable around Don. He knew all about my past and loved me anyway. There was no need for pretense and I felt a different kind of love for him. He went out of his way to make me feel special. If I'd buy him a gift, he'd get so excited as he unwrapped it, making all the right remarks, convincing me I'd chosen the very thing he wanted. When we talked, he really listened, looking straight into my eyes.

One night, he proposed.

"I love you so much," he said, "I want to spend the rest of my life with you, will you be my wife?"

I said, "Yes."

"I know you worry about your Ma and your brothers and sisters," he said, "I've been thinking about that too. I can buy a house now, and if you like, you and your family can move in there before we even get married. After we're married we could all live together. They'd be able to get away from that abusive step-dad of yours."

"Are you sure you'd want to live in a place with me and all of my family?" I asked.

He convinced me that he'd do it because he loved me. That made me love him all the more. We started making wedding plans and searching for a house. We found a small white, two bedroom house in the suburbs, with a basement for shelter in tornadoes, although it only had a dirt floor. There was a covered front porch, just right for a swing. There was even a small one car garage, and since Don was the only one with a car, it was perfect. One bedroom

DADDY NEVER CALLED ME PRINCESS

for Don and me, one bedroom for Ma and the girls. The boys would sleep on the couch. Things would be tight. But the price was right. Only $500 down.

I told Ma she'd finally be able to get away from all the abuse, if she wanted to. She was ready. The house closed. One day while Daddy was at work, we borrowed a truck, gathered up some help, and went home to help Ma pack up her life. We knew we had to hurry, in case Daddy surprised us and came home early. Hauled out his rifle.

Fall was in the air and the trees looked gorgeous, but crisp leaves were underfoot and being drug throughout the house. The neighbors had their yard decorated for Halloween with skeletons and tombstones scattered around the lawn. A black witch hung from one of the trees.

Their decorations did nothing to help the uneasy packing going on, or the somber mood.

Ma hadn't been able to pack ahead of time, so things were a lot harder. We hurried and grabbed her most important items. We had a line of people coming and going. Sheets, blankets and pillows were stuffed into garbage bags. Towels and wash rags were hurriedly wrapped around dishes. Pots and pans were set on top of other things. We held our breath with every car we heard. None of us wanted to face Daddy if he came home to see his house in shambles, although that wouldn't bother him. The fact that his family was fleeing his control, and there wouldn't be anyone to abuse, would turn him into a wild man. But thanks to all of our friends, we didn't have to confront him. We made it out safely.

Everyone headed over to the house that belonged to Don and would soon be half mine.

I lived in the new house with all my family while finishing the wedding plans.

We didn't hear a word from Daddy. We didn't want him to show up and ruin our big day. We put guards at all the doors. There were

NEW BEGINNINGS

around three hundred people at the church. I wore an off white, full length, lacy wedding gown with long sleeves and a lengthy train trailing down the back. A jeweled tiara held the bridal veil that covered my face. My sister Colleen, was my maid of honor. My sister Penny, two of my cousins and Don's sister were bridesmaids. My baby sister, Rena, was my flower girl. My brothers, Ronnie and Rodney were ushers. I stood in the back of the church and listened to the music as I watched my loved ones march to the front. Everyone looked stunning. My little sister looked so cute in her pink dress with all the ruffles and lace. A matching hat adorned her red ringlets and she carried a basket of flowers almost bigger than herself. A trail of sweet-smelling, red rose petals graced the aisle as she tossed them from side to side.

Strains of Here Comes The Bride signaled that it was my turn. I proudly walked down the aisle on the arm of my Uncle Pete. I was so happy that my family was able to share the day with us. We had a large reception and plenty of homemade food that everyone had helped to prepare. We didn't go on a honeymoon, although we did spend our first night alone in a nice motel.

Don moved in with all of us, his new family of seven. Things were tight, but everyone adjusted. I'm sure it was hard on Ma, leaving her husband after so many years and moving in with us. She never complained. Not having to worry about her getting beat up, or listening to Daddy's abuse was a huge relief.

Ma got some help with her financial situation, through Social Services. Her youngest, 3-year-old Rena, was glad that she'd be able to sleep in a bed with her Ma, and sister. Ma signed a permission slip so Penny could quit school and get a full time job at the Varsity Drive-in restaurant. I quit my job. Don didn't want his wife to work. Ronnie had to quit his job because it was too far away and he couldn't ride his bike back and forth. Rodney enrolled in a new school. There were a lot of big changes for the seven of us. We were all ready for our new beginnings.

Some man, who was supposed to be Daddy's friend, told us Daddy hadn't kept up the house payments. With a mortgage

DADDY NEVER CALLED ME PRINCESS

balance of only $500, they repossessed Ma's dream house. He also confirmed Ma's suspicions about Daddy having a girlfriend. Her name was Bertha, and Daddy had moved in with her. None of us knew where they lived. But Ma was determined to find out.

CHAPTER 35:
A TABLE FOR TWO

"Mistakes are painful when they happen, but years later a collection of mistakes is what is called experience."

- Denis Waitley

Our family of seven crowded together in that tiny house for over a year. Sometimes I thought we got on each others nerves on purpose. Don was a real perfectionist and he liked everything around him in a certain way. The plants on the table had to be turned just right. The pictures on the wall had to be perfectly straight. If anything was out of order, it drove him crazy.

Sometimes, when Don wasn't looking, the kids would move things around, just a little bit. It almost drove Don out of his mind. Maybe that's what they were trying to do.

Before we were married, people used to tell him he'd make someone a good wife. At times, I felt like he was a better wife than I was. He even liked to clean. I considered myself a perfectionist too, and I thought I did a good job of cleaning. But, on occasion, Don would go right behind me and do it again. I was glad I had a husband who was willing to help, but to go behind me and clean was taking things too far. I remember one time when I had just mopped the kitchen floor. I sat the mop upside down by the back door to dry, then went in to wash my hands.

DADDY NEVER CALLED ME PRINCESS

When I came back in the kitchen, Don had the mop and he was going over the floor again.

"What do you think you're doing? I just mopped that floor."

"Oh, I know, but you missed a couple of spots so I was helping you out."

"There was nothing wrong with that floor. But if I can't do it well enough to please you, then maybe you better mop it yourself from now on."

Of course he didn't want to take over the job. But even in other areas of cleaning, I never felt like I measured up to his expectations.

And when we got ready in the morning it would take me an hour. But Don would take a long leisurely bath, clip his nails, his clothes had to be just right and he polished his shoes, every single day. He'd stay in the bathroom for two hours. That caused a lot of problems since we had seven people who needed to get in there, and only one bathroom. Sometimes it was hard to wait. But after listening to other woman complain that their husband's were slobs, I tried to be thankful. At least I had a husband who cared how he looked.

My family liked to sit on the couch, watch TV and eat. Don wanted to sit at the table for meals. He didn't like getting crumbs all over. I didn't either, so I bought some TV trays for all of us to use. Then we tried to alternate where we'd eat, sometimes Don even used the trays.

Don and Ronnie starting fighting. Don didn't like it when Ronnie laid around the house. Ronnie didn't like it when Don tried to tell him what to do. Especially when Don complained about his lack of employment. "Quit laying around the house," he'd say, "Go get a job."

Things seemed to bother Penny most of all. She lived for fun, not to listen to Don ranting and raving. Ma was even getting restless. She started talking how much she missed Daddy, and if she only knew where he was, she might consider going back to him.

A TABLE FOR TWO

None of us were too pleased when we heard that, especially, Penny.

"No," she said, "I will not go back and live with Daddy again. Never!"

Penny had been dating an older man and he'd asked her to marry him. She needed Ma's signature, saying that she approved of the marriage, since Penny was only sixteen years old. Ma wouldn't sign. So Penny secretly devised a plan. A plan that she didn't admit to until years later. Because, no matter what, she refused to live with Daddy again. "If you can get me pregnant," she told the man she'd been dating, " I know Ma will agree to sign papers and then I'll marry you. But you'd better hurry."

Her plan worked. She came home one day and shocked everyone with her big announcement. She was pregnant. She'd never even talked about wanting a baby, like I always did, but suddenly she was having one. After convincing Ma to sign, Penny went to a Justice of the Peace, repeated vows and she was a married woman, in a little girl's body. She married a man she never claimed to love; she only used him as part of her escape. I didn't know about her plan, but I was furious at him for getting my little sister pregnant.

After that, Ma wanted to get a place of her own. She found a small apartment, right behind the house that Penny had moved into, and rented it. Ma, Ronnie, Rodney, and Rena, moved out. I wondered how Don and I would get along when we'd be alone, for the first time.

Things were peaceful, at least in the beginning. But I missed all my family. Not only was the house empty, but my soul was empty as well. My heart held a special place that could only be filled by a baby. I ached for a little one of my own.

I worried about my sister having a baby at such a young age, but she was a trouper. Even though she delivered a month early, she and her little boy came through it with no problems. I was happy for her, but my heart ached because my arms were lacking. I wished it had been me going home with a baby to love.

DADDY NEVER CALLED ME PRINCESS

Then, after all those painful tears every month, my dreams were about to come true. I was finally pregnant. Less than three months later my dreams died, along with my baby.

"A lot of women lose their first baby," the doctor said, "that's just natures way, but there's no reason you can't try again."

So we kept trying and I got pregnant again. A couple of months later, I had another miscarriage. My heart bled. I wanted a baby more than anything. The doctor could not find a reason. "You're healthy," he said, "try again."

But it wasn't happening. The doctor said I was trying too hard and that I needed to relax. But instead of relaxing, Don and I started fighting. The tension drove us farther apart. I accused him of picking fights with me because there was no one around to stick up for me. And yes, when his sister told me that someday it would be me that he screamed at, she was right. Don had a problem with anger and it showed up more every day. Although he never hit me physically, his words were like hurtful daggers. He liked to throw things.

I remember a time when I was sick. I was lying on the couch when he came in from work. Supper wasn't ready. "I'm so sick," I told him, "could you make supper tonight?"

"You want me to make supper?" he screamed, "well, I'll make supper."

He stormed into the kitchen, grabbed a can of corn and a sauce pan. He flew back in the living room and threw the corn first. The can barely missed my head. Next, a flying saucepan came whizzing by. He went back in the kitchen and got a loaf of bread, threw that and yelled, "Okay, there's your lousy supper!"

If I had felt better, I would have grabbed the stuff and thrown it right back, at least the bread. But I was too sick to argue. I never knew if he was really trying to hit me, or just scare me. The screaming matches continued and progressed. I was not one to take his angry mouth. Just like Ma, I couldn't shut up. I always fought

A TABLE FOR TWO

back. After we cooled down, we'd both apologize, and things went well. I still wanted to be with him, more than anywhere else. I trusted him completely, and I was determined to make our marriage work. One divorce was heartbreak enough. Don and I had been having some good days and things were really great between us. But Ma seemed determined to put a damper on things.

When Don went to work in the morning I'd drop him off at the factory, so I could keep the car. Then I'd either go shopping or visit Ma. I liked to visit her except when she was drinking. Ma liked her beer, but when she was drunk, she acted like a little kid, she could be cruel.

"I know something you don't know," she'd chant to me, "but I'm not gonna tell ya."

"Well what is it that don't want to tell me?" I'd ask.

"Oh, nothing," she'd say.

"Then why do you keep bringing it up?"

"Oh, I don't know, sometimes, I can be mean."

And she could, just like all of us, but it was usually only when she was drinking. I'd hear those same words, every time she got drunk, but she never gave a hint as to what she was talking about. Until I pressed her one day. "I'm tired of hearing that all the time. Either tell me what you want me to know, or quit saying that. Now what are you talking about?"

"Oh, nothing. But you'd better be careful, you know you can't trust any man."

And then she added something new.

"But if I told you, you'd leave Don tonight."

I got a sick feeling in the pit of my stomach. Try as I might, I couldn't get any more out of her. I felt so hurt, anytime she said that. After all, one of the reasons she told me that Don would make a good husband was because I could trust him. Then I'd get mad,

183

DADDY NEVER CALLED ME PRINCESS

thinking that just because she'd had such bad luck with the men in her life, was no reason for her to cast doubts on the man I married. Maybe Don and I did fight sometimes, but it was just as much my fault as it was his. And I had no intentions of leaving him.

Maybe Ma needed someone else in her life, then she'd leave mine alone. Don had an uncle who was single, and just the right age. He had been living out of state, but he'd recently moved back. Maybe I'd see what I could arrange.

CHAPTER 36:
HE'S BACK

"Sad endings begin every new romance."

- Unknown

"How would you like to go on a double date with us tonight, Ma?"

"Oh, all men are the same. None of them are any good. You can't trust a one of them."

"Well, I can. I trust Don. Wouldn't you like to go out and dance with someone besides me and him for a change? After all, it's been over two years. Don has an uncle. His name is Floyd. He's never been married and he wants to meet you." After a little convincing, she agreed to go.

Don and I were ready and picked up Ma at her apartment. She walked out the door wearing a bright red dress, covered in lace, with a wide gold belt, long dangling earrings and high heeled spikes with open toes. She looked sharp and sexy like she always did when we went out. The overpowering scent of her Tabu Cologne filled the car.

We headed over to pick up Floyd at his apartment. Don pulled in the drive, blew his horn and a big, stocky guy walked out. He had blond hair and blue eyes, wore black dress pants, and a solid blue dress shirt. Ma and Floyd both looked pleased at what they saw in each other.

DADDY NEVER CALLED ME PRINCESS

They seemed to hit it off from the beginning. There was a lot of laughter coming from the back seat. Don pulled in at The Wagon Wheel Bar. The guys were real gentlemen. They ran around and opened the doors for Ma and me. The evening was spent dancing and listening to country music until the bartender announced last call.

Before dropping them off, Floyd invited all of us to go out the following Friday. Ma talked about Floyd all week. She admitted they had fun together and couldn't wait to go dancing again. Ma's long awaited Friday couldn't arrive soon enough for her. Floyd picked everyone up in his 1968 Mercury Montego. The blue, two-door hardtop, still had that brand new-car smell, even though it was a few months old by then. After that, they started going out alone. Ma seemed happy and I was glad to see her find some joy in her life.

But someone else had caught wind of the new romance. Daddy. He must have been jealous because he started calling Ma.

"You better watch him," we all tried to warn her.

"We were together for over twenty years." she said, "and I can't help it, I still love him."

None of us could talk her out of it. They went dancing and she called me the next day, sounding all giddy.

"Oh, we had a lot of fun. He's changed so much."

"You're flirting with danger, Ma. And isn't he still living with Bertha?"

"Yeah. Now she can see what it feels like to be the other woman, instead of me."

The situation seemed to be reversed. Us kids used to go out and leave Ma at home worrying. Now she was going out, and we were the ones to sit home and worry.

Penny called me after another of Ma and Daddy's dancing dates.

HE'S BACK

"Guess what?" she said. "Ma and Daddy are wanting to get back together. Ma told him she wouldn't go back with him unless he'd ask her in front of Bertha."

"You've got to be kidding."

"No, and Daddy agreed. He's supposed to pick Ma up tonight and take her to his house so he can tell Bertha. Ronnie and I are going to follow them so we can find out where he lives. You know Ma would never remember."

We both laughed, agreeing that Ma was so terrible with directions.

"Well you two be careful. Hard to tell what he'll do if he catches you two spying on him."

They got the address without being spotted. We waited anxiously for Ma to return home safely. Later that evening, Penny called in a frenzy.

"Daddy beat Ma up! Right in front of Bertha. I heard a car and ran to the window. Daddy leaned over and opened Ma's door, shoved her out then took off before I could get out there."

"Well that no good. Is Ma alright?"

"She's all bruised and bleeding, but I don't think she has any broken bones. She won't go to the hospital."

Don and I took off to Penny's. Poor Ma looked a sight. Her dress was torn and splattered with blood. She was so mad, she could have chewed nails.

"He's gonna pay for this," she said. "He wanted me to leave all you kids and run off with him. Can you imagine? I told him I wouldn't do that. He said Bertha loved him so much that she got rid of all her kids, just for him. He wanted to know if I loved him enough to do that. And Bertha," Ma spit out the words, "just stood there in shock, looking dumb-founded."

Right in the middle of Penny's story, we heard a car pull in. We

DADDY NEVER CALLED ME PRINCESS

ran to the window and saw Ronnie. He stormed through the door repeating a string of not so nice words about his dad. He'd somehow gotten ahold of Daddy's number. He called and his anger took over.

"You beat our Ma for the last time, you S.O.B. And you're never going to hit her again. Meet me at the bar downtown and I'll show you what it feels like to get beat up."

"Bring it on," we heard Daddy scream. "No son of mine is ever going to whip me!"

They agreed to meet. Ronnie grabbed a ball bat and rushed towards the door.

"Wait for me," Penny said. Their car threw gravel on the way out the drive.

We stayed there and waited with Ma, wondering if we should call the police. Ma didn't want us to. And, knowing her, she'd never press charges against him. Ronnie had been wanting to make Daddy pay for years. He was so full of anger, who knew what it would take to pull him off, once he got started. We could only envision the worst.

When Ronnie and Penny came back they both looked fine. "Well, what happened?" I asked.

"Oh, the coward never even showed up," Ronnie said.

"We figured he was probably hiding out at some other bar." Penny added.

We stayed for awhile and made sure that Ma was alright. When the excitement died down for the night, Don and I headed home.

Before going to bed, I got another call from Penny.

"You'll never guess what happened now," she said.

"Nothing would surprise me."

"Well, Ma insisted that I take her over to Bertha's. We stood on the front porch and beat on the door til she opened it, but she

HE'S BACK

wouldn't let us in. That open door was all I needed. I forced my way in. Bertha started arguing with me and Ma went into the bathroom. She was in there quite a while, but as soon as she came out, she was ready to leave. But I wasn't. I was still yelling. Then Bertha screamed and said if we didn't leave right that minute, she was going to call the police and have us thrown out. Well here's what I think of you calling the police," I said, "and I ripped the phone out of the wall and threw it on the floor. Then Ma and I stormed out of there. When we got in the car I found out why Ma was in such a hurry to leave. She had ripped the curtains off the window, tore the shower rod down, sprayed shaving cream on the mirror and all over the walls. She trashed the bathroom real good. You know Ma."

"Well, that sounds like her," I said. "Maybe she got it out of her system and she can settle down now."

"I hope so," Penny said, "she acted happier when she was going out with Floyd."

We talked for awhile, then I was hoping to unwind before bedtime. We said our good-byes. Don disappeared into the kitchen. I could hear the microwave running. He came back and handed me a cup of frothy hot chocolate.

"Made with love for you, Little One."

Sometimes he could be so sweet. He served it in my favorite mug, with miniature marshmallows floating on top. We relaxed, talked, and enjoyed the evening until bedtime, and beyond. And no matter what, there was no place I would have rather been, than in Don's arms.

The next day, Don called his uncle Floyd and tried to explain things. Floyd tried to be understanding and, since he really liked Ma, he came back. They started going out again. I was hoping he'd help Ma get over Daddy so she wouldn't get hurt so much. My mind focused on getting those two together. I had them over for dinner several times. There were plenty of nights out dancing, with the four of us, and them alone. As Floyd started taking up more of her time, I could see the relationship growing between them. Her heart

DADDY NEVER CALLED ME PRINCESS

seemed to be leaning more towards Floyd. She even talked about filing for divorce.

And all the dates did wonders for Don and me. With everything that had been going on, I hadn't been worrying about trying to get pregnant. And that's when it happened. I was overjoyed to learn that I was pregnant for the third time. And I felt so positive. I just knew that would be the one. The baby I would hold in my arms. Please God?

CHAPTER 37:
LITTLE TINY TEARS

"A baby will make love stronger, days shorter, nights longer, bankroll smaller, home happier, clothes shabbier, the past forgotten, and the future worth living for."

- Anonymous

    Things were going well, except for the morning sickness, but I was even glad for that, it meant a little baby was growing inside me. I passed the dangerous first three months, started gaining weight and wearing maternity clothes. I was so proud and hopeful. The more I gained the better I liked it, everyone could tell by looking that I was pregnant.

    Nothing could take away my happiness.

    I was eight months along when my world fell apart, not because of the baby, it had to do with my husband. I'd never suspected that I couldn't trust him, it's the one thing I was always certain of. I was absolutely shocked to hear the things that Ma accused Don of. She told me that Don had made some very suggestive passes at her, and other family members, when I wasn't around. Being in total shock I tried my best to sort things out before Don came home from work. I couldn't understand, believe or make sense about anything I'd heard. I confronted Don and he denied everything. Maybe there had just been some misunderstandings. Maybe he was only being friendly and they took it the wrong way. How was I supposed to know what really happened? I didn't want to deal with another

DADDY NEVER CALLED ME PRINCESS

failed marriage and I was about to have his baby.

I wanted so bad to believe him. So I convinced myself he was telling the truth and nothing was ever meant by what they thought he'd done. I told him I'd forget about it as long as I didn't hear about anything like that, ever again. He promised that I wouldn't. We tried to go on as if nothing had happened. I tried to focus on the baby about to be born.

Ma gave me a baby shower and I loved all the sweet baby gifts. The crib was ready. Don and I had taken Lamaze classes together and everything was in place for our new little one.

Having only one week to go my doctor gave me an examination.

"You're in labor," he said, "you're already dilated two. You need to get to the hospital."

Suddenly fear, and excitement beyond words hit at the same time. I called Don, then picked him up from work. He drove home, grabbed my suitcase and we headed for the hospital. After several hours of labor, with not much happening, the doctor told Don to go home. "Try to get some sleep," he said, "we'll call you if anything happens." Just before he was ready to leave my pains started getting harder and closer. Things happened fast. Within the hour, and thirty-six hours after I'd checked in, I heard the cry of our baby. We had a little girl. Nothing has ever thrilled me more. I was ecstatic. She was worth every pain. "You mean that's it?" I said, "I just had a baby? That wasn't as bad as I thought it would be." Of course it was painful but compared to all the horror stories I'd heard through the years, it was not unbearable.

Our little girl weighed 6 pounds 11 ounces. She was perfectly healthy except that she was born with Clubfeet: both of her feet turned inwards. The doctor said it may have happened because she was born breech: feet first. She had to have cast put on both of her legs, from her toes to her thighs. When the casts came off, she had to wear special shoes, held together with a steel bar, for several hours daily. But she was so good natured, nothing ever bothered her.

We named her Lynn. Don cried when he saw her for the first time. She was such a wonderful baby. She never cried unless she needed something. I didn't think there was ever a sweeter baby in all the world. My dreams had finally come true. I was a mother. My very own baby to love and no one could ever take her away from me. Now that we were a family of three we'd no longer be sitting at a table for two.

As a little girl, the one thing I wanted most of all for Christmas, but never got, was a Tiny Tears Doll.

"Now," Ma said, "you have your very own "Tiny Tears."

Oh, how we loved our little girl. Those first few weeks, even when I got up through the night for her feedings, I didn't mind losing sleep, I had a baby and she was worth anything. I'd hold her close and rock while feeding her, then I'd sing a lullaby and put her back to bed.

She smelled so sweet after her bath. I'd wrap a towel, turbine style, around her head and snap a picture as she laughed. I'd rub baby lotion all over her then put footie pajamas on that squirming little body. We'd snuggle while I read. Or, if it was morning, I'd dress her in something cute. She had just enough dark hair so that I could wrap a curl around my finger, right on top of her head. Then I'd put her in her Daddy's arms and make sure my camera had film for the shot.

I loved to sew and many soft flannel nighties rolled off my machine. We bought her plenty of toys and rattles, bottles and booties, lots of adorable dresses, a stroller, a high chair, a walker, an infant seat, a swing and a playpen to keep her safe.

My heart filled with joy when she smiled at me for the first time, at four weeks old. And when she was five and a half weeks old she started cooing. I loved to cuddle and kiss her little fingers and play with her toes. During the times she was able to have her special shoes off she'd smile and coo while I massaged her tiny feet. When

DADDY NEVER CALLED ME PRINCESS

she was asleep I'd go in to check on her, just to make sure she was still breathing and that I wasn't dreaming.

Once, I even put a wig on her, just for fun, and she laughed so hard as I clicked the camera for another picture. Anything new that she did warranted another snapshot.

For her first Easter I made her a little basket and set in on the table, surrounded with grass, more candy and toys. Then I set her right in the middle of it and took her picture.

Her uncle Rodney loved her to pieces and he made a wonderful babysitter, when I could drag myself away from her long enough to go anywhere.

Life was good. I kept a well stocked supply of film, and looked forward to Lynn's exciting milestones every day. When she was six and a half months old, I heard the word Ma for the first time, followed by Da Da, and then Mama a month later. Lynn made my life complete. I was full off joy and hope.

Suddenly it was October first. Don and I would celebrate our fourth Anniversary. He was working and I was at home with the Baby. Ma was there visiting with us.

I had an uneasy feeling because she had brought her own six pack and was on her last can of beer. She was looking a little glassy eyed. She wouldn't eat anything. I couldn't even convince her to drink a cup of coffee.

"I need to talk with you, Wanda," she said. "this is hard for me to tell you, but it's important and you need to know."

My heart began pounding as I listened to her.

"I can't let this go on any longer," she said. I sat there with a sinking feeling in my soul.

"Don has always tried lots of sexual stuff with me. I tried to ignore him. I didn't want to hurt you. The night after you had Lynn, Don came over. He'd been drinking and wanted to know if I'd have a beer with him to celebrate. I was alone and I told him I didn't want any. He looked like he'd had enough already. He started messing around. He tried to reach out and fondle me. He kept grabbing himself between the legs, talking dirty. All of a sudden he grabbed me, pushed me back over the table and pulled at my clothes. He intended to rape me. I was struggling and trying to fight him off but he was too strong for me. Thank God, Ronnie pulled in the drive. When Don heard his car he let go of me and away he went. I didn't tell Ronnie what had happened."

I can't say that I was completely unaware, but I never suspected that it had gone that far. I couldn't deny it any longer. I knew I couldn't live like that and I had to leave him. There was no use talking to Don, he had denied it last time, yet it continued to happen. The only person I knew who had a truck was Buddy, so I called on him. He was heartbroken and going through a divorce himself at the time. He worked second shift so I was hoping he would be available to help. He didn't even ask questions. He willingly came over. He'd even stopped and picked up a load of boxes. He helped me pack up life for my baby and me.

I found a cheap, two-room, upstairs apartment, close to Ma. The only bathroom was down the hall, and Lynn and I had to share that with the older couple in the next apartment. But we managed. The only joy through all of it was my little girl, Lynn. The hardest part was taking her away from her dad, and I missed him terribly too, but trust is everything. And I couldn't live with anyone who would do such a horrendous thing.

Someone told me to talk to a professional. I cried through the entire meeting. She suggested marriage counseling but Don refused. He didn't want strangers knowing our business.

I applied for and received financial help. They thought it was better for a mother to stay at home with her children, and I agreed. I couldn't imagine the thoughts of someone else watching my baby as she grew and did all the first things that I would miss. I had no money to file for a divorce and could not even entertain the thoughts of getting another one.

DADDY NEVER CALLED ME PRINCESS

But this time I wasn't alone. Lynn was just starting out in the world and I needed to be brave for her. We could face anything together, just me and my little "Tiny Tears." My daughter gave me plenty of reasons to get up in the morning. Then, after several months, we were both finding an outside reason to smile. Our lives were about to take on a new turn.

CHAPTER 38:
MY BEST FRIEND

"When it hurts to look back and you're scared to look ahead you can look beside you and your best friend will be there."

- Maggie Lee

Another divorce would break my heart, I couldn't force myself to file, even though Don and I had been separated for almost two years. Buddy had been there for Lynn and me, even during his own trials. He helped us through all the hard times, and I tried to repay the favor. He had four sons but none of them ended up living with him. I could not fathom taking Lynn away from her real dad. A step-dad raised me and I didn't want that for her. At one point I even went back with Don to see if we could try again. Buddy also went back with his wife for the same purpose. We tried to work things out with our spouses, but it only showed each of us that some things were just not meant to happen. Divorce was inevitable, for both of us, but we became best friends as we tried to help each other deal with the pain.

Time passed. Ma filed for divorce and it was granted. Daddy married the woman he'd been living with. Ma also fell in love with Don's Uncle Floyd and they were married.

The relationship between Buddy and I continued. Somewhere along the way, our friendship turned into love. He asked me to marry him. I was afraid to try marriage again, so we tried living together. That didn't work, I couldn't take all the guilt, so we got

DADDY NEVER CALLED ME PRINCESS

married. We vowed to love each other until death. He started calling me Angel Face, although I was certainly no angel. As happy as I was I still felt like something was missing in my life.

"Is there another man?" Buddy asked.

"No, I assured him, "you're the only man for me, I can't explain it, but somethings missing." Lynn loved her new daddy as much as he loved her. But I wanted to give Buddy a child of ours. I figured that was the missing ingredient, then we'd all be happy.

I got pregnant but just a few weeks later I had to endure another heartache. I lost the baby. "Just try again," the doctor said.

I got pregnant again, and I lost that one too.

Lynn seemed all the more precious and I felt so blessed to have her, but I wanted to give her a brother or a sister. Then I got pregnant again. The first three months were critical and each day seemed to drag. Then what I had dreaded most came about. I started spotting and cramping. But that time the doctor prescribed a prescription for progesterone and complete bed rest.

"Just put your feet up and watch the boob tube," he said.

Buddy treated me like a queen. He took over all the household chores, along with his job in the factory. My brother, Rodney, offered to come over and give us a hand on many occasions.

I was over visiting Ma one day. "You know," I told her, "Rodney is so good with Lynn, she just loves him. He even cleans house, almost as good as I do."

We heard a knock on the door and Rodney walked in, grinning from ear to ear.

"Well," Ma said, "speak of the devil and look who walks in."

"Guess what?" he said, "someone from church came to my door. I talked to them and I asked Jesus into my heart, I got saved."

"Oh, I'm sure," Ma said as she laughed. Rodney just smiled.

And then, only two months later, Ma made a rare visit to

church. She asked Jesus into her heart too. Ever since that day she was after me to go to church with her. I could come up with more excuses, just to keep her off my back.

My pregnancy continued until I only had five weeks to go. Something woke me around 1:00 a.m. Wow, it was hot in there and we didn't have air conditioning, only a fan that sat on top of our dresser. I felt drenched from head to toe but I had never been known to sweat that much. It was even hard to breathe. My commotion woke my husband.

"Boy, it's hot. I'm sweating buckets over here." he said.

I forced my swollen body out of bed and I got a surprise. "Honey, my water broke!"

"What!" he said, as he climbed out of bed and stood beside me.

I was so scared, it was too early, I couldn't be in labor.

"Don't worry, Angel Face," he said, "it's gonna be okay. I'll call your mom and tell her we're on our way to drop Lynn off, then I'll get you to the hospital."

Nothing ever bothered him, he was great in a crisis, the exact opposite from me.

We dropped Lynn off at Mom's and headed for the hospital. After being prepped and given a hospital gown, I was lying in bed and Buddy was sitting in a chair beside me. Would our baby be okay? "Please, God," I prayed, "I'm so afraid."

Buddy and I had taken Lamaze classes and he was doing a great job of being my coach. He timed my pains, rubbed my back and handed me ice chips, all the while trying to convince me that everything would be fine.

"Ouch! Get the doctor," I yelled, "this babies coming."

They made Buddy leave, gave me a quick exam, then wheeled me to delivery.

"Push, push," I heard, and our little girl came into the world.

DADDY NEVER CALLED ME PRINCESS

But I didn't hear the sound that all mother's wait to hear, their babies first cry. She wasn't breathing. Doctor's were rushing around but they weren't telling me anything. Then I got a glimpse of her just before the nurses whisked her away. She looked blue. "Please, God?"

I heard a little sound before they disappeared, weak, but it was still a cry.

They finished my care and wheeled me into the hall. I met Buddy and told him that we had a little girl. He was ecstatic. "But something's wrong," I whispered, "and they took her away for tests." Nurses wheeled me to my room while Buddy walked beside us. The doctors kept our baby while we waited for news, but it wasn't good.

"Your little girl has hyaline membrane disease," the doctor said, "her lungs are not fully developed and we don't know if she'll make it through the night."

I gasped as I remembered that was how President Kennedy's baby had died.

The doctor sent Buddy home, "Maybe you can both get a little sleep," he said, "come back in the morning, we'll know more then."

Before Buddy left we both prayed. "Please, God, let our little girl live. Breathe life into her tiny lungs and we'll start going to church." We weren't really interested in going before, but we were desperate.

After a long, restless night, Buddy was back with me. We held hands as we nervously waited for news. The doctor walked in and he was smiling. "She's a little fighter," he said, "she'd never make it otherwise. She'll have to stay in the hospital and we'll keep a close eye on her until she gains some weight, but I think she'll be okay."

We were both so relieved. God heard and answered our prayers.

I went home with empty arms but our little girl was doing fine and already gaining weight. We named her Pamela Sue, but Buddy

MY BEST FRIEND

called her our little "Kitten."

Not too long after we were able to take Kitten home.

Then Sunday came. We kept our promise and went to church.

After trying several churches we found one where we felt comfortable. After the service they were inviting people to come forward and give their hearts to Jesus.

"We've all sinned," the pastor said. "Even if we've only sinned once, we're still a sinner. Even if we've only killed once, we're still a murderer." I had never committed murder but I was certainly guilty of sinning more than once.

The pastor continued, "Our sins nailed Jesus to the cross. He paid the price so that we could go free. All we have to do is accept the payment that He made. To spend eternity in hell, just do nothing. Jesus loves you. He will forgive you and make you a new person, in Him. You will go to heaven someday, and you can live each day on this earth with the joy of the Lord."

We had been in that church once before, and again, I felt an overwhelming urge to go forward. Buddy must have felt the same pull because he reached for my hand.

"Come on, Angel Face," he said, and nothing could hold us back. With my hand in his we walked forward together. Buddy went with a man and I went with a woman to a private room in the back. She showed me from the Bible what it meant to simply give your heart to Jesus.

"God, I know that I'm a sinner," I prayed, "and the wages of sin is death-separation from God, in hell forever. I believe that Jesus died on a cross, was buried and rose again. He died in my place to pay the penalty for my sins. I'm sorry, please have mercy upon me. Forgive me, and come into my heart, for Jesus' sake."

I left the room feeling like a giant weight had been lifted off my shoulders. Buddy said he felt the same way. As best friends, hand in hand, we had opened our hearts to the Savior. Our lives would

DADDY NEVER CALLED ME PRINCESS

never be the same. God not only erased our past, but He changed our entire world, past, present and future, for all eternity. We hadn't even been searching, but He had found us, Jesus, our new best friend.

CHAPTER 39:
A NEW NAME

"But now thus saith the Lord that created thee, O Jacob, and he that formed thee, O Israel, Fear not: for I have redeemed thee, I have called thee by thy name; thou art mine."

- Isaiah 43:1

    Have you ever waited in line to get picked for a game? Waiting with your heart pounding to hear your name being called? Wondering who was going to get picked before you? Or worrying that someone you couldn't stand would choose you? Worrying whether you were even going to get chosen at all? feeling like no one wanted you? I remember waiting in line and wishing I could disappear.

    All my life I longed for Daddy's approval. I only wanted him to notice me or call me a sweet name like Princess. Anything besides illegitimate. Even though that never happened, something better did. There's a new name written in heaven, just for me. God not only calls me "Princess," but He calls me His child, Daughter, Christian, The Apple of His Eye, Beloved, Precious, and many other wonderful names. I never felt like I was worth anything, but no matter what I've done in the past, God claims me. He thinks I'm worthy and it has made all the difference in the world. Buddy and I told everyone we loved about our new "Best Friend."

    God allowed me the privilege of witnessing to my immediate family. Within a few months each one of them had asked the Lord

DADDY NEVER CALLED ME PRINCESS

into their heart. I've had a problem with low self-esteem ever since I was a little girl. But I finally discovered from my heart, not just my head, that God loved me. He would never love me any more because of anything I did. He would never love me any less because of anything I failed to do. He didn't love me because of me, but because of who He is. Therefore, I could relax, be myself, and stop worrying what other people thought of me. I was free to allow God to love them through me, and that changed my life. I finally found out what had been missing, the Lord.

Time passed, Rodney found the girl of his dreams, Debbie, and they were married.

Our girls were growing. Kitten had a head full of natural curls, just like her sister. I loved to watch their pony tails bounce as they played and laughed together. Kitten was such a little chatterbox. She had a special kind of laugh that spread joy to any one close. She was also walking and following her big sister everywhere. Lynn acted like a little Mother.

Then I found out that I was going to have another baby. I wondered what was ahead. But I wasn't the only one carrying a new life. My baby brother, Rodney, and his wife, were expecting a baby of their own. It didn't seem possible that my little brother was going to become a daddy, but he loved kids, and I knew he'd make a wonderful dad.

My pregnancy flew by without any problems. We were right in the middle of another hot summer and I woke up at 3:00 a.m. in labor, but it was only eight days early that time. Buddy took charge, got everything under control, and dropped the kids off at Ma's. I felt safe and loved around him. He calmly drove to the hospital, never going over the speed limit.

Two hours later I welcomed our perfectly healthy little boy into the world, weighing in at almost eight pounds. My first red-headed baby and we named him Trevor.

Three weeks later Rodney and Debbie's baby entered the world, a perfectly healthy little girl with a head full of natural red curls.

A NEW NAME

They named her Rachel.

As the months went by the kids grew. Lynn started first grade and life was good.

None of us ever heard from Daddy. The kids had never even met their grandpa. Then, before we knew it, another two years had flown by and Christmas was upon us. Trevor would be two that year, old enough to really enjoy the holidays along with his sisters.

We decided to have our family Christmas party early, before things got too hectic. The gathering was at Ma's. She had plenty of room and a pool table in her basement. The party was fun, with lots of laughter, games, prizes, food, and plenty of pictures.

My brothers were both great mechanics and we heard lots of talk about their new plans. They were going to open their own garage and go into business together. They were trying to come up with a name for their shop. We all knew that our brother's garage would be a great place to take our cars. We could trust that our vehicle's would be fixed right for an honest price.

After the party, back at home I busied myself with our own family traditions. The kids helped me make several batches of cookies. I also made Buddy's favorite peanut butter fudge.

We spent time searching the woods for just the right scotch pine to trim together while drinking eggnog and singing. I sewed costumes for the kids so they could be in church plays.

I had to shop for some last-minute gifts, with Christmas only a few days away, so I fought the crowd at the mall. I returned home to find our world turned upside down. I walked into the house and put my armload of packages on the table. Buddy's voice and a look on his face dampened my holiday spirit.

"You better sit down." he said.

"Why? What's the matter?"

"Ronnie called. Rodney's been in an accident. On his way home from work he was hit head-on by a drunk driver in a truck that had

DADDY NEVER CALLED ME PRINCESS

crossed the center line. They don't know if he's going to live through the night."

"Well, that's Rod, it's impossible! He's only twenty-three."

Sensing my shock, Buddy handed me my Bible. I opened the pages at random and read the first passage I came across: "Then shall the dust return to the earth as it was: and the spirit shall return unto God who gave it." Ecclesiastes 12: 7

I was speechless. Was the verse trying to tell me something about Rodney's future?

Buddy stayed home with the kids while I jumped in the car and took off for the hospital. I met up with Rodney's wife, Debbie, and Ronnie with his wife. Ma couldn't face the reality. She stayed home and prayed. I leaned on the strong arms of my step-dad, Floyd, for support.

Under treatment in intensive care, Rodney was only allowed a couple of visitors at a time. Ronnie went in first. He came out looking as if he'd been stunned by an electric shock.

"Wanda, you don't want to go in there. Rodney doesn't even look like himself. They have so many machines hooked up to him. He's losing blood faster than they can pump it back in."

I stayed out in the waiting room and tried to pray. But I really didn't know what to pray. They said Rodney had brain damage. If he lived, he would be like a vegetable. We stayed together through the night. Along towards morning, I left, in a daze. I wanted to stay longer at the hospital but I thought Buddy needed the car so he could go to work.

Back home I was totally worn out and emotionally drained. Buddy did go to work and I went in and laid down on the bed. I couldn't go to sleep. I kept praying. Suddenly, unexpected peace settled on me and I relaxed. "Rodney will be alright." I said out loud. A glance at the bedroom clock showed 10 a.m.. My body calmed down and I fell sound asleep.

A NEW NAME

The phone woke me four hours later. Our pastor was on the line with news about my brother. The family had given him permission to pray that God's will would be done with Rodney. As soon as the prayer ended the alert sounded on the life-support machine. Rodney simply discarded his useless body, as he might an old overcoat, and went on without it, to heaven, for a new one. With his next breath he was in the Lord's presence, at exactly 10 a.m.

I hung up the phone and burst into tears. Family called and our house turned into a flurry of people coming and going. We knew that no matter how it happened, Rodney had finished his work on earth and God had called him home. How did we feel about the man who had hit Rodney? We got word that he was beside himself with grief for what he had done. Our pastor said it had been an accident and that is just what God used to get Rod home. We forgave him.

Then we had to plan a funeral. We ran into a huge problem. The funeral director needed at least $3000 to start making arrangements, and if we didn't have it, they couldn't even bury Rodney. None of us had that kind of money and we didn't know how to get the cash.

Ma's heart was absolutely crushed to think that she would not even be able to bury her son. They would keep him, somewhere, until we came up with the money. We all gave what we had, some even begged neighbors for a loan, or anyone we could think of. With God's help the money came in that was needed. Us kids were going to make all the arrangements, Ma couldn't handle being there. Just before leaving for the funeral home, Penny got a phone call from Ma. "Your dad just called," she said, "He's going to meet you at the funeral home."

"We haven't seen him in almost ten years," she yelled, "and he doesn't need to be there."

"Now calm down," Ma said, "if he shows up, don't say anything. Maybe he wants to pay some of the money, if he does, let

DADDY NEVER CALLED ME PRINCESS

him. Then we can give the money back to everyone."

We headed to the funeral home, and sure enough, Daddy showed up. We tried to be civil. We made all the decisions while Daddy sat there in silence. The funeral director asked, "And how do you want to pay for this?"

Daddy spoke up, "I'm going to pay for it."

"How much are you going to pay?"

"All of it." Daddy said. He pulled out his check book and wrote a check for the total amount, over $7000.

"Later, at home, Ma said, "it's about time he finally did something for his son."

We met back at the funeral home for the first showing with all of the immediate family. Rod was supposed to be ready at 6:00 pm. We got there a little early and the funeral director told us, "Just wait in the break room, I'll come and get you when he's ready." Six o'clock came, then 6:15, then 6:30. We were still waiting. Penny was biting her nails, pacing, and on her second pack of cigarettes. The funeral director finally came in.

"We can't let you see him yet, he's still not ready."

"Well why not?" Penny said, "he was supposed to be ready a half hour ago."

When they told her that Daddy had to approve it first, she lost it.

"He has no right," she screamed."

"Yes, he has the right because he paid the bill. And he requested that no one see him until he gets here."

"Well, he hasn't seen his son in 10 years. Even now he's late. And he's not going to stop us. That's my brother. If you don't let me see him, then I'm going to go to every room in here. I'll open every flipping door in this building until I find him." She jumped up and jerked the door open, ready to storm through the funeral home.

A NEW NAME

Daddy was standing there.

The funeral director said, "they want to see him."

"OK, now now, calm down," Daddy told Penny. "I just wanted to be the first one to see him so I could make sure he looked alright."

He finally led us to our brother and Ma's beloved son. We held each other and sobbed.

It was a big funeral. Rodney had lots of friends. Daddy came alone. We were glad he was able to hear the pastors great salvation message. We prayed that God would work in his heart. Five people accepted Christ as their Savior, Daddy was not one of them. They played Rodney's favorite song, "When the Roll is Called Up Yonder, I'll be There." Rodney had received a new name, given by God, four years earlier. Rodney's new name had been "called up yonder" and there was no doubt he was "there."

Losing our brother was a horrible shock and we missed him terribly. But we had followed Rodney's example and asked Jesus into our heart's too. Rodney was the first one in the family that God called home. God's grace assured us that, one by one, we would someday follow Rodney to heaven. God gave each of us a peace in our hearts that we couldn't understand, but God's peace comforted us. Rodney's death brought all of us closer to the Lord and each other.

A few days after the funeral Penny heard from Daddy again, another demand.

"How come no thank you cards have been sent out yet?"

"I just buried my brother," she said, "and you're worried about thank you cards?"

"Well, I had friends who sent flowers. And when do you guys plan on paying me back for the money I spent on the funeral?"

"You ain't getting nothing from us. You didn't do anything for him in 23 years. I may be your daughter, but you were never a dad,

DADDY NEVER CALLED ME PRINCESS

only a sperm donor. What are you going to do? Take us to court to get the money? Well if you do, then you'd better be ready for a fight."

CHAPTER 40:
THAT'S MY DAUGHTER

"That feeling you get when you suddenly realize that you were fighting for nothing all along."

- Gina Faye

    Daddy didn't try to collect the cost of the funeral from us. But we read in the paper where he took the man who had killed Rodney to court. Daddy won his case. The man had to reimburse Daddy for the cost of his sons funeral. That was the last thing we'd heard from, or about him, in over 8 years. Until that day in 1986. I had stopped at Penny's house to visit. As soon as I walked in she handed me a steaming mug.

    "Here," she said, "sit down and drink a cup of coffee. Have I got a story for you!"

    "This must be a good one," I said as I pulled out a chair, sat down and took my first sip.

    "Oh yeah, it is. You're not going to believe what I did."

    "Okay, so don't keep me in suspense."

    "Well, I was sitting in a dimly lit bar, at one of the round tables, with my boyfriend, Harry. The door opened, I looked up and turned to Harry, "I think that's my dad."

    "So was it Daddy? After all these years?"

    "Yes. he walked in with one of his friends and sat down, a few

DADDY NEVER CALLED ME PRINCESS

tables away. I wasn't sure at first, but after I got a better look, I knew it was him. I walked over to their table. Daddy looked up, smiled, turned to his friend and said, 'That's my daughter.'"

"'Your daughter?'" His friend pulled out a chair, nodded to me, and told me to sit down and he'd buy me a drink. Okay," I said, "but I'm here with my friend, Harry."

"'Well, tell him to come on over.'" he said. "'I'll buy you both a drink.'"

"I was thinking, *this is a big mistake*. But I motioned for Harry to join us."

"'So what are you drinking?'" he asked.

"Oh, I'll have a whiskey and water." I told him. "Harry ordered a draft. We took turns buying rounds till we were all feeling pretty good. Daddy's glassy eyed friend looked at me, and said, "'I didn't know Red even had a daughter.'"

"Yeah, Daddy's friends always did call him "Red."

"Well that's better than a lot of names I could think of to call him." she said with a chuckle. "So I told him, Well, what a surprise that he never mentioned me. Did he also forget to mention the fact that he has two more daughters and two sons?"

"'Um-mm, I guess he did.'" He said with slurred speech. "'But if you're his daughter, can I ask you a question?'"

"Go ahead," I told him.

"So he started talking, real slow. "'Why haven't I ever seen you before? With everything that Red's been through. Where were you when he had all his surgery's? Where were you when he spent all that time in the hospital?' I was getting madder by the minute. That man didn't know what he was talking about. The Jukebox was playing, "Diggin' Up Bones," by Randy Travis. You know, that song that talks about resurrecting hurtful memories from the past. I couldn't hold it in any longer. The anger overpowered all my childhood fears. That unsuspecting friend was about to hear some real truths about the man he thought was so great."

"Oh no. So what did you say?"

"Everything I could think of. I looked him straight in the eyes and let loose. Well," I said, "where were you when he let his kids go hungry? Sometimes we couldn't even go to school because we didn't have anything for lunch. Yet he never went hungry. He came home every night and made Ma get up and cook him a steak. If she didn't feel like getting up at 3:00 in the morning, he'd slap her up the side of her head with his steak, pull her out of bed and jerk her to the kitchen. And then there were all the times he came home drunk and beat the living daylights out of her. If you were such a great friend, where were you then?"

"Wow, I bet he was shocked."

"Oh yeah, his eyes bugged out. Daddy just sat there and never denied a thing. I was so loud that the barmaid came over and asked Daddy if he wanted to have me kicked out."

"'No,' Daddy told her. She'll be quiet.'"

"Like heck I will," I said, "I ain't gonna be quiet. I've been quiet for too many years."

"If she only knew the half of it."

"That's for sure. I just kept remembering all those things Daddy used to do and I couldn't shut up. I told him everything I could think of, on the spot. Then, when I'd think of something else, I'd start in again. I glanced at myself in that big mirror behind the bar and I looked like a wild woman. That only spurred me on."

"And I'm sure it didn't take much to do."

"You got that right." She laughed. "So I just kept screaming. I told him about the time we had been eating nothing but beans for a week. We walked 2 miles to the store & returned some bottles, so we could have some bread to go with our beans for Thanksgiving dinner. Ma found out later, accidentally from her neighbor, that Daddy went to her house and ate a Turkey dinner. I asked him

DADDY NEVER CALLED ME PRINCESS

where he was when Daddy didn't put clothes on our backs? I told him about all the kids at school laughing and making fun of us, calling us poor little kids, asking us why we wore the same old clothes all the time, or why we didn't have any shoes to wear."

"Were people staring at you?"

"I didn't notice if they were. I was too mad. I just kept right on yelling."

"So then what did you say?"

"I said, don't try to condemn me. Don't judge me. Where was our dad when we needed him? He made good money. But he chose to sit in the bars and buy rounds for all his friends. His family did without. Would you do that? Is that the kind of a man you want for a friend?"

"Sounds like you let him have it with the full force of anger that's been escalating for years."

"Well, I guess I did. The man just stared at me with his mouth open. Daddy never even dared to say a word. He knew I was telling the truth. He just sat there and listened to me rant for over thirty minutes. Then I started winding down."

"You mean the wild red-head finally ran out of things to say?"

"Ha. Ha. But then I could hear the clink of the pool balls in the background. Daddy looked at me with a rather sheepish grin. Then he glanced at his friend, and said, '"That's my daughter.'" So I finished my drink, got up and walked out. And boy, did that ever feel good. That was the first time I'd ever faced Daddy without being terrified of what he was going to do. And I certainly didn't start crying just because he looked at me. It was getting pretty warm in that bar. The cool night air cleared my head. I even thought of more things I could have said."

"I know how you feel. I can think of a lot of things to say, after it's too late. And what was Harry doing all that time?"

"He just sat there, listening to me. When I walked out he was right behind me. I even told him that I should go back inside for seconds. He didn't think that was a good idea. But, Oh well, I feel better than I have in years. And I wasn't trying to be mean. I didn't throw bar stools or anything. He just made me so mad. I was only stating the facts."

"I know, Daddy used to tell people that you were an instigator. He ought to know, he probably thinks you're too much like him."

"Well, like father, like daughter. Maybe he got a little taste of his own mouth. I wonder how he liked being on the other end for a change."

"Oh, I'm sure he wasn't expecting anything like that. You probably surprised him big time. I wonder what they talked about after you left? And what about all those hospital visits? What kind of surgeries did Daddy have?"

"I don't know. I didn't stick around long enough to find out. But he looked okay to me. It couldn't have been anything too serious, or someone would have gotten ahold of us. I guess we'll just have to wait and see. I wonder how many years will go by before he shows up again?"

CHAPTER 41:
NO LONGER AFRAID

For God hath not given us the spirit of fear; but of power, and of love, and of a sound mind.

- 11 Timothy 1:7

"Hey, Penny, someone's at your table."

Penny worked the night shift as a waitress. She grabbed a napkin, walked over to the table and set it down in front of the patron. She found herself looking into the eyes of Daddy. None of us had seen or heard from him in around 7 years. They started talking, catching up on life, then she invited him over to her apartment that week-end. She asked me to come along.

Penny and I were sitting at her apartment, waiting for Daddy.

"Tell me what he's been doing the past several years?" I asked Penny.

"After being diagnosed with sugar diabetes, many years ago, his health steadily declined. He lost sight in one eye and needed a transplant. He had problems with his circulation and needed many surgery's. First they cut off his toes on one foot and didn't find any blood to circulate. The next surgery cut up to his ankle but that still wasn't enough for blood circulation. They had to cut up to his knee before they found blood. He eventually had both legs amputated and ended up with artificial legs. He bought a van, then paid a fortune to have it customized so he could drive with hand controls.

DADDY NEVER CALLED ME PRINCESS

He also has one of those fancy electric power chairs."

"Wow, that's really too bad," I told her, "it sounds like he's been through some rough times. Has he changed any?"

"Not that I can see, he's the same loud mouth drunk he's always been."

"How did you feel about seeing him? Did any of that old fear come back?"

"Nope, he doesn't scare me now. Since they cut his legs off I can run faster than he can." As we laughed we heard a car pull up so we ran to the window.

"Here he is," Penny said, "and he came alone."

We went outside to meet him. He didn't look like a big, powerful man anymore. Watching him maneuver his frail body out of the van and into his chair was not a pretty picture.

We all went back inside. Penny motioned Daddy to the best seat in the house, her comfy over-stuffed chair. We sat on either end of the couch. Penny served coffee and chocolate cake to everyone, I pulled out my Canon and captured it all with a click.

"Still like taking pictures?" he asked.

"Sure do," I said, "smile."

We showed him photos of all his grand kids, an even dozen at that time.

"Well, this one looks just like me," he said, "red hair and all."

Daddy asked how Ma was getting along. He seemed genuinely interested as we told him that she had married Floyd and they were doing great.

Penny asked questions about his artificial limbs. He was eager to take his legs off for an inspection by us. They looked and felt so real.

"Hey," Penny said, "Did you ever forget that you didn't have

NO LONGER AFRAID

your legs on and tried to jump up then fell flat on your face?"

"Well," he said, "as a matter of fact, I did do that once." We all laughed.

After a couple of hours Daddy was getting ready to leave. He invited us over to his house in the suburbs for the following Friday. We told him we'd try to come and visit. We knew he lived there with Bertha, and we didn't want to hurt Ma by going. But when we mentioned it to her later, she didn't seem to care either way.

Penny picked me up on Friday. We went to visit Daddy. We pulled up in front of a small white house with blue shutters. Daddy was sitting on the porch in his power chair, waiting for us. He seemed so pleased that we came. He showed us around outside first, demonstrating his scooter as we walked. Their house was on a city lot with a couple of shade trees, a small garage, and some hedges along the drive. Red geraniums bloomed in the window box and some purple petunias trailed down the sides of a whiskey barrel.

We went back in the house. Penny had met Bertha before, but Daddy introduced me to her. She seemed very submissive and eagerly did whatever Daddy told her to do. I wondered if she had suffered any beatings from his hands.

Daddy showed us his Ham Radio studio. The entire room was filled, wall to wall, with all his equipment. Bertha stayed in the living room and waited, then she served coffee and cake.

"Well, I got a shocking phone call a while back," Daddy said.

"Oh yeah," Penny said, "and what was that all about?"

"A man told me about some woman in a nursing home. She wasn't doing very well and she was asking to see me."

"So, did you go? Who was it?" Penny asked.

"Yeah, I went," Daddy said. "It was my mother."

"Your mother?" we both asked at the same time. We knew the

DADDY NEVER CALLED ME PRINCESS

story about the day she asked her kids if they wanted to go for ice cream. She dropped them off at the orphanage instead. She never went back. They were all raised as orphans.

"And what did you say to her?" Penny asked.

"Well, I don't know, what do you say to someone you haven't seen in over seventy years?"

Daddy didn't want to talk about his mom anymore. And since we'd already been there a couple of hours we figured it was time to leave. We promised to keep in touch.

Sometimes, after that day, Daddy showed up where Penny worked. He'd stay and visit for awhile. He even brought Bertha with him a few times. Penny got to know her a little better.

Before we knew it a couple more years had slipped away. Penny got a phone call from Bertha. Daddy was in the hospital and he was asking to see his kids. Maybe he was feeling guilty and wanted to make amends for all the abuse he'd dished out through the years.

Ronnie, Penny, Rena and I went to see him in the hospital. They would only let a couple of us visit at a time. I went in with Penny. Daddy was lying in bed.

He looked so puny, weak, and worn out. Nothing like the powerful, robust man who had, over the years, instilled undeserving fear in all his family. No longer tough and loud, but quiet and defenseless. He was so thin we could see his fragile bones protruding from his hospital gown. His face was a pale gray color. For the first time, I didn't even want to take a picture. But at least he was aware and able to talk. He looked up and smiled, then focused on me.

"Hey, Wanda, I see you're still wearing your class ring."

"Yes, I never take it off." If he only knew how much that ring meant to me. Time passed with mostly small talk and everyone's main subject, when they can't think of anything else, the weather. Then we had to leave so Ronnie and Rena could visit. We promised

NO LONGER AFRAID

to come back in a few days. I felt so guilty. I knew that one of us should have told Daddy about the Lord, but I hadn't been able to say a word.

Penny got another call from Bertha. Daddy was slipping fast. If we wanted to see him alive, we'd better hurry. All of our family prayed that Daddy would ask Jesus to forgive him, as all of us had done many years earlier. As long as his heart was still beating, there was hope. We were praying we wouldn't be too late to tell him about the Lord, since we'd both chickened out last time. As hard as I tried, somehow I wasn't able to get the words out that I knew he needed to hear, they seemed to stick in my throat.

The night before we got the call I had a dream that Penny told Daddy about the Lord. Everything was so vivid, even down to what Penny was wearing, and when she picked me up that day, that's exactly what she was wearing. I told her about my dream.

"Well, she said, "apparently that means I'm the one to tell him. I'm not afraid, but what am I supposed to say?"

I pulled a pamphlet out of my purse that described the plan of salvation. "Here," I told her. "You can just read this to him if that would be easier."

Penny and I went to the hospital and they let us go in together. Daddy was on life support by then. The machine with all the lights, noise and numbers seemed to dominate the room. The strain of the last few days had weakened him. He looked much worse.

"I need to talk to you," Penny told him. "This is important and they won't let us stay long. So I hope you'll listen. But I guess since you can't talk, then you'll have to listen." She laughed. "Ma and all of us kids have asked Jesus forgiveness for the things we've done wrong, and we're praying that you'll do the same thing. We want to know that we'll all be together again in heaven someday. Do you know that you're going to heaven when you die?"

He nodded his head yes, then held up his hand, and we noticed he was wearing a Masonic Ring. He had been a member of the

DADDY NEVER CALLED ME PRINCESS

Masons for years. He pointed to his ring.

"No," Penny said. "That ring won't get you to heaven. But there is a way that you can know, for sure. Just ask Jesus to forgive your sins. Thank Him for dying on a cross for you, and ask Him to come into your heart. Jesus loves you and He's waiting for you."

Daddy couldn't speak, but we saw a tear roll down his cheek. Penny took his hand.

"If you understand and want to do this just squeeze my hand."

I'm sure Penny's heart was racing, like mine. We watched Daddy squeeze her hand.

"Just repeat these words after me in your mind," she told him as she read the pamphlet.

She asked him afterwards if he had prayed the prayer with her. He nodded "yes," and if the look in his eyes was any indication, he had just opened his heart to the Savior.

"And you better not be lying about this," Penny told him, "because when I get to heaven, you better be there!"

I was so glad that God had waited. We hadn't been too late. God had used Penny to tell Daddy and we cried tears of joy. God had brought a powerful, strong, robust man, to the end of himself before he finally gave up control and asked the Lord to take over. We'd finally get to know our dad as the man he could have been, if he'd asked Jesus to help him, years ago.

But then, all too soon, we heard a voice over the loud-speaker.

"Visiting hours are now over."

We had to leave so others could come in. Penny and I said our good-byes. Daddy not only looked old and tired, but his face radiated a new look of contentment and peace. He waved to us from his hospital bed. I knew he was only waving to his daughter Penny, but just to be sure, I let her walk ahead. Then I turned and peeked back around the curtain. I was the only one he could see.

NO LONGER AFRAID

His eyes were smiling. And then Daddy waved, just to me.

Walking away from that hospital room I felt as if I was walking on clouds. My heart was light and free of the past hurts that Daddy had inflicted. Because of God, I could love Daddy, in spite of his human frailties.

We couldn't wait to tell Ma and the others about Daddy's decision to accept the Lord. We all rejoiced, knowing that God is long-suffering. He had answered our prayers and waited for Daddy to ask forgiveness and invite Him in.

With a phone call from Bertha the next day, we knew that he was also free from pain, fear and earthly cares. He was in the Lord's presence. Daddy was no longer an orphan. He was a child of the King.

Arrangements were made and Penny offered to pick Bertha up and give her a ride to the funeral. All of us kids went to say good-bye to a Daddy we never really knew on earth, but we had no doubts that we'd get to know him some day, as a changed man, in heaven.

Daddy was also a World War 11 Veteran in the United States Army. So to honor those who served, he was given a military funeral. Some of Daddy's friends came and were surprised when they saw us. They didn't even know "Red," as they called him, had any kids. On the way to the cemetery, the funeral procession was stopped by a train.

"Well, look at that," Bertha said, "he got held up by the train, one last time. Every time we passed this way, your dad got held up by the train and he always hated it."

Honor guards folded and presented the U.S. flag to his wife Bertha. We listened to the playing of Taps by a lone bugler. We heard the gun salute. One last salute and then it was over. We walked quietly towards the waiting limousine.

Back at the funeral home we climbed into Penny's car and headed over to Daddy's house. Bertha rode with us. Penny was

DADDY NEVER CALLED ME PRINCESS

going to drop her off, but whether Bertha liked it or not, I knew that wasn't the only thing Penny planned on doing.

CHAPTER 42:
HOPE THROUGH THE VALLEY

For I am persuaded, that neither death, nor life, nor angels, nor principalities, nor powers, nor things present, nor things to come,

Nor height, nor depth, nor any other creature, shall be able to separate us from the love of God, which is in Christ Jesus our Lord.

- Romans 8:38-39

Bertha invited us in and pulled out some folding chairs. She sat there fidgeting, biting her nails, and pulling at her hair. We listened while she tried to share memories of Daddy. "I have something for you kids," she said, like it was Christmas. She gave Ronnie a small set of tools. Penny got Daddy's cufflinks, and a pen with his name on it that he had received from the Masons. She gave Rena some small trinket. I didn't get anything.

Penny looked at me, squinted her eyes, and I knew Bertha was in for a fight. If she thought a few little trinkets would satisfy Penny, she was wrong. I knew Penny was planing to take Bertha to court in order to get her fair share of Daddy's estate.

Ronnie went in to look around Daddy's Ham Radio room. He came out carrying Daddy's lock box. Bertha didn't have a key, so Ronnie broke it open. The box was not full of money, and it didn't contain a hidden stash of food. What we found inside brought tears. Daddy had some well-chosen mementos from his family. The first thing we spotted was a picture from the day him and Ma got married. They were standing in front of a decorated car with their

DADDY NEVER CALLED ME PRINCESS

arms around each other. They both looked young and happy. Right under the picture was Ma's wedding band from Daddy, all bent and worn, and the face of an old watch of hers. Rodney and Rena's birth certificate was also in there, and a few pictures of all his kids. One picture was of Rodney and Rena, with their arms around each other. There was a check stub from Ronnie's very first job, and a check stub that Penny had received from The Varsity. And my heart rate quickened when I found, last of all, the receipt with my signature for the $50 couch I had bought Ma.

He had saved those small treasures for many years and threatened anyone who dared to look in his private box. Why did we have to find clues that he cared, only after he was gone?

Well, it was nice of you kids to stop by," Bertha said, "thanks for coming."

"Oh, that's okay," Penny said, "I'll be back." And I knew that she meant business.

Life went on and it was good. Penny called me one night.

"Guess what I just heard on the radio?" she asked.

"Beats me, what did you hear?"

"There's a new song out by Randy Travis, called, "The Box," and it sounds just like us."

I couldn't wait for the radio to play it so I went right to the store and bought the CD. In the song he talked about finding a box full of mementos after his dad died. One of the lines goes, "We all thought his heart was made of solid rock but that was long before we found the box." What a perfect time for us to find that particular CD. It brought many good feelings.

Penny hired a lawyer to fight for Daddy's estate. "He didn't do anything for us his whole life," she said, "and if there's anything I can get, even if it's only a thousand bucks, I'm going to take it." I would not be included in Daddy's estate since I was not his legal child.

HOPE THROUGH THE VALLEY

Bertha's name was not on anything, and she wasn't too happy with Penny getting a lawyer.

"Well I would have given you anything," she said, "all you had to do was ask."

Yeah, right. But by then everything was in the hands of the court system and we knew that could drag on for quite awhile.

But life was busy for everyone. All of us were happily married with families of our own, but it hadn't always been that way. Each of us girls had married abusive men, or men we didn't love, then, after enduring much anguish and suffering, we all went through painful divorces. Some of us even repeated the cycle and married abusive men for the second time. We seemed to end up with men just like Daddy. I went through the heart break of two divorces before I married Buddy, a wonderful man. Early in our marriage we had both met Jesus and He changed our lives. And Buddy reminded me of Uncle Pete: kind, caring, gentle and loving. Buddy and uncle Pete both acted more like a Christian before they were saved, than some people do after they're saved.

Ronnie, had married the love of his life, Alonda, over twenty-seven years earlier, and they were still together. Our hectic lives were filled with raising kids, working and trying to make our mark in the world. We were all doing well, with eleven boys and six girls between us.

But one thing was on all of our hearts. We had lost touch with Rodney's daughter, Rachel. Her mom had moved out of state, right after Rodney was killed. They had moved a few times and we had lost touch with them. Other than a couple of pictures we had received when she was little, none of us had seen her for almost twenty years. But I continually prayed that she would get saved. I knew Rodney wanted his daughter to be saved, so they'd meet in heaven someday, and since he wasn't able to tell her, I wanted to tell her for him. But God had His perfect plan all worked out, in His perfect timing.

My brother, Ronnie, got a call one day, from Rachel. She had

DADDY NEVER CALLED ME PRINCESS

tracked him down from the Internet. He gave the number to Penny, she called Rachel back and found out that she was living several hundred miles away, in Florida. Plans were made, a plane ticket was purchased, and Rachel was on her way to Michigan. The plane landed and oh, what a reunion that was. We all wondered if she'd look like her dad. Well, looking at her was almost like seeing Rodney all over again. We found out that she had two children back at home. The only downside was that she was with living with an abusive man. She talked freely about him and the things she told us were heartbreaking. He was waiting for her back in Florida, so she wouldn't be able to stay too long. She'd be staying with Penny. Rena and I would gather at Penny's so we could all visit together.

Rachel had never been as cold as she was in Michigan's November weather. And since she had never seen snow, we were hoping that maybe we'd get a blizzard before she had to leave. She filled us in on her life, we gave her some mementos from Rodney that we'd been saving. Penny gave her a canvas that Rodney had painted. He named it, "Our Wedding." There were two doves, wedding bells, and two hands at the bottom, wearing wedding rings. Everything was surrounded by red roses. He had painted their names and the date of their wedding in the center.

I had saved, among other things, some of Rodney's hand written answers to the board games we used to play, where you write your deepest thoughts. It was hard to part with, even after twenty years, but Rachel needed it more. Maybe she could see a small part of her dad's soul.

Rachel did not know the Lord, but she seemed open and interested when we talked about Him. I invited her to church with me. "Maybe," she said, "sometime."

Penny, Rena, Rachel and I dressed up and took her to visit Ronnie. When we walked in, and he saw how much Rachel resembled Rodney, he was wiping tears away. We all had a great visit and came away with many pictures before we headed back to Penny's.

HOPE THROUGH THE VALLEY

Penny taught Rachel how to sew, how to do ceramics, and they did plenty of cooking and baking together. We all crammed a lot into those few short days until Rachel had to leave. She was disappointed because we didn't get any snow while she was there. But Penny told her that she was included in Daddy's estate and she would need to come back up when that was settled. We said our good byes and promised to keep in touch.

Penny's attorney finally called with a court date. Rachel was notified and came back in March of 1998. She was able to see snow for the first time. She loved the blanket of white stuff. Penny, Rena, Rachel & I dressed for the cold and spent time outside. We showed her how to make snow angels and have snow ball fights. They wrestled in the snow while I stood back and bravely took pictures.

The estate was finally settled. Bertha received the biggest share, the remaining shares went to Daddy's four kids. Since Rodney was no longer living, his share went to his daughter, Rachel. Each of them received just over $7000 each and I was happy for them.

Penny, Rena and Rachel came to visit me, just before Rachel needed to head back home. They were all smiling mysteriously. "Hey, you guys," I said, "What's up?" Penny handed me a thick envelope. When I opened it a stack of hundred-dollar bills was inside, along with a letter. This is what she wrote:

Remember when we were young, the days were long and there was no fun?

Daddy would come home drunk, and we would hit the bunk.

Sometimes it was late and he'd be mad because we'd hibernate.

He was always mean and never gave us any green.

Then the years passed by and Daddy died and we all cried.

Then we said, "now that he's dead, know what would be funny? If we got all his money!"

He was our Daddy, that fact is true, but of course you considered him Daddy too.

DADDY NEVER CALLED ME PRINCESS

So here's a little something from us to you.

Love always,

Penny, Rena and Rachel

I was so surprised. Tears fell freely as I hugged and thanked all of them. They had included me and I felt like a part of the family.

Rachel took her money, she hadn't decided what she wanted to do yet, and bought a plane ticket home. We even found out that she had a freezer bag full of snow in her suitcase.

Penny took her share and bought a food wagon. She turned it into a booming business and runs it to this day. She sets up at baseball games and auctions, just to name a couple of places. So if you're ever running around and see "WILLIE'S WIENIE WAGON," buy a hot dog and say "Hi," to Penny.

Everyone used their money wisely. I tried to put mine to good use too, but their one stipulation was that I couldn't use it to pay bills. They knew me all too well. They said I had to use it for fun. And for me, nothing would be more fun than a new camera. So, after pouring over Consumer Report magazines, I bought a brand new Canon SLR camera, along with some extra attachments and several rolls of film. Then I was ready and waiting for our next family get-together, dreaming of all the pictures I'd take. Our family always shared a big Thanksgiving dinner with all the trimmings, closely followed by a big Christmas celebration. Watching everyone unwrap their gifts would be a great time for taking photos. And then again, I could take more pictures when we celebrated everyone's birthdays. The list was endless.

My camera got a work out and life took over. Then, in July of 1998, Rachel came back. She brought both of her kids with her, and her mom, Debbie. We had a fun time as we reminisced with Debbie, and got to know Rodney's grand children. We thought Rachel would be heading back to Florida, that is until then she made her big announcement. She had decided to move up to Michigan with her kids. And, she was two months pregnant. She

HOPE THROUGH THE VALLEY

was trying to get away from the man who abused her. Penny helped her find a small apartment nearby. Rachel's mom left to go back home. We enjoyed our annual Christmas celebrations with Rachel and her two kids.

In February, on Rena's birthday, Penny and I had the once in a lifetime privilege of watching the miracle of birth. We were in the delivery room when Rachel's little boy was born. It was awesome. I have pictures to prove it. They both came through with no complications.

When Rachel got her strength back she told us that she'd had enough of our cold Michigan weather. She was moving back down south. The father of her kids also convinced her that he had changed and wanted her back. But before she left, God allowed me to witness another miracle. He had been working in Rachel's heart. She called and said she wanted to go to church with me. Buddy and I picked her up, along with her three kids, and we all went to church on Sunday. Then, after many years of prayer, God answered that day. Rachel got saved. A week later she was baptized. I had the joy of watching the beginnings of her love for the Lord. She'd reach for her Bible every day, like a life line. She was just starting to discover how much God loved her and that He had a plan for her life. I was sure that Rodney was singing around the throne, in the presence of the angels. After too short of a time, she had to leave.

Later, I received a picture of Rachel, smiling, holding all three of her kids. She was finally away from the man who had abused her so horribly. The Lord spoke to her heart and gave her the strength to walk away, for good. But she wasn't alone anymore. Rachel never had an earthly father to love. I had an earthly father, but was never given his love. Yet we both had the all encompassing love of a heavenly father, as did all of our family. His love is given without merit or condition. It is a love that protects and desires to work all things together for our good. A love that brings hope and a future without fear. In this love we find approval, not because of anything we have done, but because of what has been done for us. Without question, His love changes everything.

Do you need help finding hope and healing from your own abusive situation?

Contact Wanda at http://wandasmaxey.com